TANKS

OF WORLD WAR TWO

Colour plates by Jean Restayn

Text by Jean Restayn, François Vauvillier, Yves Buffetaut, and Philippe Charbonnier

1939: BLITZKRIEG

1940: WAR IN THE DESERT

1941: THE EASTERN FRONT

1944: FRANCE

1945: THE FALL OF THT REICH

1939
BLITZKRIEG

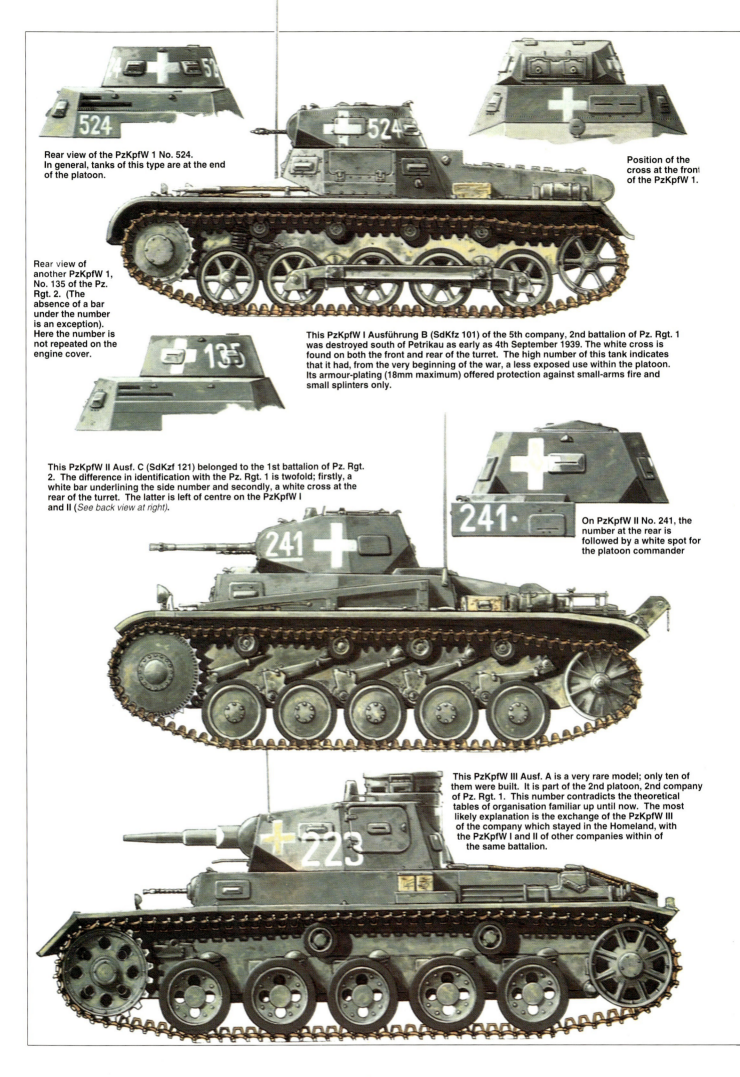

Rear view of the PzKpfW 1 No. 524.
In general, tanks of this type are at the end
of the platoon.

Position of the
cross at the front
of the PzKpfW 1.

Rear view of
another PzKpfW 1,
No. 135 of the Pz.
Rgt. 2. (The
absence of a bar
under the number
is an exception).
Here the number is
not repeated on the
engine cover.

This PzKpfW I Ausführung B (SdKfz 101) of the 5th company, 2nd battalion of Pz. Rgt. 1
was destroyed south of Petrikau as early as 4th September 1939. The white cross is
found on both the front and rear of the turret. The high number of this tank indicates
that it had, from the very beginning of the war, a less exposed use within the platoon.
Its armour-plating (18mm maximum) offered protection against small-arms fire and
small splinters only.

This PzKpfW II Ausf. C (SdKzf 121) belonged to the 1st battalion of Pz. Rgt.
2. The difference in identification with the Pz. Rgt. 1 is twofold; firstly, a
white bar underlining the side number and secondly, a white cross at the
rear of the turret. The latter is left of centre on the PzKpfW I
and II (*See back view at right*).

On PzKpfW II No. 241, the
number at the rear is
followed by a white spot for
the platoon commander

This PzKpfW III Ausf. A is a very rare model; only ten of
them were built. It is part of the 2nd platoon, 2nd company
of Pz. Rgt. 1. This number contradicts the theoretical
tables of organisation familiar up until now. The most
likely explanation is the exchange of the PzKpfW III
of the company which stayed in the Homeland, with
the PzKpfW I and II of other companies within of
the same battalion.

PANZER-DIVISION IN POLAND, 1939

The white cross made an ideal target, so it was soon either covered in mud or repainted in grey (with slight differences of shade) or scratched and faded in various ways.
The 1. Pz. Div. never used yellow paint for its crosses.

A PzKpfW III Ausf. D (SdKzf 141), armed with a 3.7cm gun but equipped with a weak armour-plating. It belonged to the 2nd company 1st battalion of 1. Pz.Rgt. This tank was to be put out of combat on 16th September 1939 near Bzura by a direct hit in the track wheels, right-hand side. Rapidly repaired, it was able to participate in the end of the campaign.

Position of the cross at the front of the PzKpfW IIs.

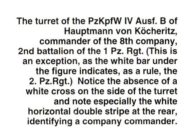

The turret of the PzKpfW IV Ausf. B of Hauptmann von Köcheritz, commander of the 8th company, 2nd battalion of the 1 Pz. Rgt. (This is an exception, as the white bar under the figure indicates, as a rule, the 2. Pz.Rgt.) Notice the absence of a white cross on the side of the turret and note especially the white horizontal double stripe at the rear, identifying a company commander.

Rear view of another PzKpfW II, Nº. 311 of a platoon commander (white vertical bar) of the 3rd company of Pz.Rgt. 1.

A PzKpfW IV Ausf. A (1935 model) of the 4th company, 1st battalion of the Pz.Rgt. 1. The white cross and the tank number (2nd tank from the 1st platoon of the 4th company) are repeated at the rear of the turret. The PzKpfW IV was the best tank used by the Germans in Poland. Its only weak point was its extremely thin armour-plating which, on the Type A, was only 20mm at the front and 15mm on the sides.

Position of the formation sign on one of the rare PzKpfW Is still used by the division in May-June 1940.

Different types of nationality markings:

a) Balkankreuz visible on the majority of tanks which took part in the Polish campaign: large white old-style narrow cross partially repainted with inside lines in Panzergrau.

a

b) Balkankreuz of the shape adopted for newly manufactured tanks delivered after the Polish campaign (mainly the PzKpfW III Ausf. E and F.)

b

c) Cross appearing on the roof of some turrets for aerial reconnaissance.

c

A PzKpfW I of the 3. Kp (1st platoon, tank No. 4) of the Pz.Rgt. 1. It is the only fighting company of the 1. Pz. Div. still equipped with several tanks of this type.

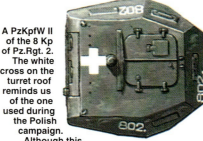

A PzKpfW II of the 8 Kp of Pz.Rgt. 2. The white cross on the turret roof reminds us of the one used during the Polish campaign. Although this aerial reconnaissance cross was frequent, its use was not widespread.

A PzKpfW II Ausf. C of the II. Abteilung of Pz.Rgt. 2. (5th company,1st platoon, tank No. 4). The Balkankreuz is painted in white on a Panzergrau background. On the turret the white cross is filled in.

Position of the oak leaf sign at the front of the turrets of PzKpfW II, seen here, tank 201.

Examples of the numbers on some of the PzKpfW IVs of the 4th company of Pz.Rgt. 1.

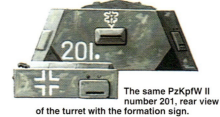

The same PzKpfW II number 201, rear view of the turret with the formation sign.

Side view of the PzKpfW II Ausf. C number 201 (H.Q. 2nd company) of the I. Abteilung Pz.Rgt. 2. The point following the number is typical of this regiment.

The exact shape of the 1.Pz.Div. formation sign in 1940.

PzKpfW III Ausf. E of the 7th company (2nd platoon, tank No. 3) of the II. Abteilung of the Pz.Rgt. 1. Although of modern conception for its time, this tank, with its 30mm armour and a 3.7 cm gun, was inferior to many French tanks. However the fact it had a radio more than compensated for any structural weakness.

PzKpfW III Ausf. E of the Kompaniestab of the 1st company of I. Abteilung of the Pz.Rgt. 2.

Rear view of Nº 101. From this angle there is no full-stop (an exception to the rule). The oak leaf situated at the rear is repeated at the front right.

A Panzerbefehlswagen III of the II. Abteilung of the Pz.Rgt. 1, tank commander Hauptmann Gittermann. This command tank was found within the Abteilungstab.

The white bar underlining the number (see above and below) is distinctive of the II. Abteilung of the Pz.Rgt. 1.

The sign of the 1.Pz.Div. often appeared on the front plate of the turret on the PzKpfW III and IV.

The tanks of the 8.Kp. of Pz.Rgt. 2 all bear an insignia at the front of the turret.

Top of the turret of a PzKpfW IV of the 8 Kp. of Pz. Rgt. 2, tank Nº. 813.

PzKpfW IV of the I. Abteilung of the Pz.Rgt. 1. The tanks of the 4. Kp. had no turret roof cross or formation sign.

This rear view of tank Nº. 411 illustrates an interesting difference in the shape of the figures within the same company.

A PzKpfW IV Ausf. C of the 4.Kp. (2nd platoon, tank Nº. 3) of the I. Abteilung of the Pz.Rgt. 1. There is no Balkankreuz at the rear of the tank. With only 28 mm of armour-plating this tank was very fragile. It compensated for this weakness by a 75mm short-barrelled, yet rather inaccurate, gun.

GERMAN TANKS OF THE 3. AND 4. PANZERDIVISIONEN, 1940

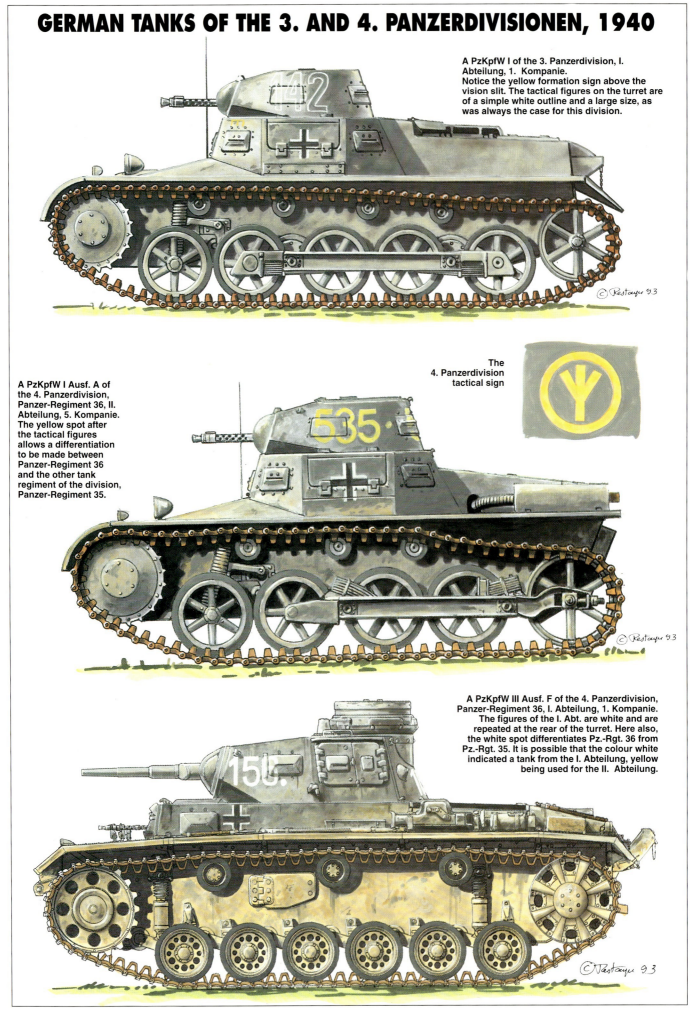

A PzKpfW I of the 3. Panzerdivision, I. Abteilung, 1. Kompanie.
Notice the yellow formation sign above the vision slit. The tactical figures on the turret are of a simple white outline and a large size, as was always the case for this division.

The 4. Panzerdivision tactical sign

A PzKpfW I Ausf. A of the 4. Panzerdivision, Panzer-Regiment 36, II. Abteilung, 5. Kompanie. The yellow spot after the tactical figures allows a differentiation to be made between Panzer-Regiment 36 and the other tank regiment of the division, Panzer-Regiment 35.

A PzKpfW III Ausf. F of the 4. Panzerdivision, Panzer-Regiment 36, I. Abteilung, 1. Kompanie. The figures of the I. Abt. are white and are repeated at the rear of the turret. Here also, the white spot differentiates Pz.-Rgt. 36 from Pz.-Rgt. 35. It is possible that the colour white indicated a tank from the I. Abteilung, yellow being used for the II. Abteilung.

This PzKpfW 38 (t) of the 7. Panzerdivision belonged to the I. Abteilung, (2. Kompanie) of Oberst Rothenburg 's Panzer-Abteilung 25. At the beginning of the May 1940 campaign Rommel's division had 106 PzKpfW 38 (t) out of a total of 219 tanks. This PzKpfW 38 (t) has, like all other Panzers of the division, large red tactical figures outlined in white.

An sIG 33 SPG of sIG-Kompanie 705 (7. Panzerdivision). Unlike tanks, these 150mm self-propelled guns do not have the large red tactical figures outlined in white. sIG Kompanie 705 was then posted to Schützen-Brigade 5. Another gun of the same unit was called "Bismarck", the letter B no doubt corresponding to a battery. Particularly surprising for a self-propelled gun, the gun mount was installed complete on board the SPG, including its original wheels.

A PzKpfW IV Ausf. D of the 3. Panzerdivision, I. Abteilung, 4. Kompanie.

TANKS AND ARMOURED CARS OF THE 7. PANZERDIVISION, FRANCE 1940

This PzKpfW I of the 7. PzDiv. is painted in grey. It belongs to the 1. Abteilung, 1st company. This is more of an armoured reconnaissance vehicle than a tank; because of its weak armour and because it was not heavily armed, it was only to have a minor role.

A SdKfz 231 of the 7. Pz.Div. More of an armoured truck than a real all-purpose vehicle, this armoured car was to be rapidly replaced by an eight-wheel version.

Detail of the marks painted on the armoured car. In yellow, the formation sign, in white, the tactical sign of a Panzerspähwagen Kompanie.

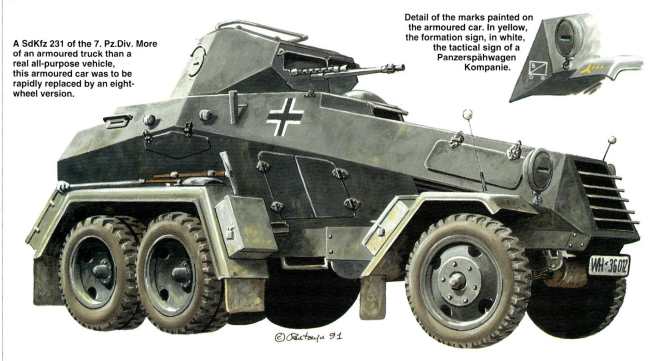

A Skoda 38 of the 7. Pz.Div. An excellent and very reliable tank, it was the type preferred by Rommel in difficult terrain. Its armament was highly efficient in 1940. The well-conceived chassis was to be used throughout the war, and until 1974 by the Swedish army.

Detail of the formation sign painted on the PzKpfW 38 (t) Hull.

TANKS OF THE 3. AND 9. PANZERDIVISIONEN, 1940

A PzKpfW II of the 3. Panzerdivision, II. Abteilung, 5. Kompanie
The figures are painted in broad white contours on a Panzer grey background.
The 3. and 4. Panzerdivisionen were part of the Panzerkorps of General Hoepner in Belgium.

The 3. Panzerdivision tactical sign.

Panzerbefehlswagen I (observation and command poct) of thc Beobachtungzug of the 9. Panzerdivision, in the Netherlands. The formation sign, a double yellow cross, could easily be confused with that of the 6. Panzerdivision, therefore it was permanently removed after the French campaign.

PzKpfW IV Ausf. D of the 9. Panzerdivision, I. Abteilung, 4. Kompanie.
Notice the unusual position of the tactical number. Each division personalised its units by using figures of a different size and colour and in a different position.

Tactical sign of the 9. Panzerdivision.

THE 6. PANZERDIVISION

A PzKpfW IV of the 6. Pz.-Div. This was the best tank fielded by the Germans in 1940. Its armour and its excellent 75mm gun made it a formidable opponent.
But they were not in sufficient numbers to play a decisive role in the battle.

Detail of the marks painted next to the hull machine gun.

A PzKpfW II of the 6. Pz.-Div. Tank belonging to a 1st company.

A Skoda PzKpfW 35 (t) of the 6. Pz.-Div (65. Pz.-Abteilung). This unit attacked a French line by surprise in the Brunehamel region (50 km to the west of Monthermé). After some hard fighting, a thousand French soldiers were captured.

Detail of the formation sign painted on the front of the hull.

PANZER IIs IN 1939-40

A PzKpfW IIc of the 1. Pz.Div (5. Pz.-Rgt), tank commander Feldwebel Hans Voigt; in the Sedan area 14th June 1940, during fighting south-west of the town. No formation sign. Above, detail of the rear of the turret.

A PzKpfW IIb (SdKfz. 121) of the 4.Pz-.D. During the fight for Warsaw the tank was destroyed and the crew killed. The turret number is white, the yellow cross outlined in white is repeated at the rear of the hull, with the unit sign.

Details of the rear engine cover with the white strip for aerial reconnaissance

A PzKpfW IIc of the 2. Kp of the Pz.Abt.z.b.V.40 during combat in Norway. Three companies were sent for the invasion of Scandinavia. One was equipped with three famous Neubaufharzeug, used mainly for propaganda purposes.
Above: details of the rear of the turret, the tactical sign V is repeated at the front of the hull.

HALF-TRACKS AND TANKS OF PANZERKORPS GUDERIAN, FRANCE 1940

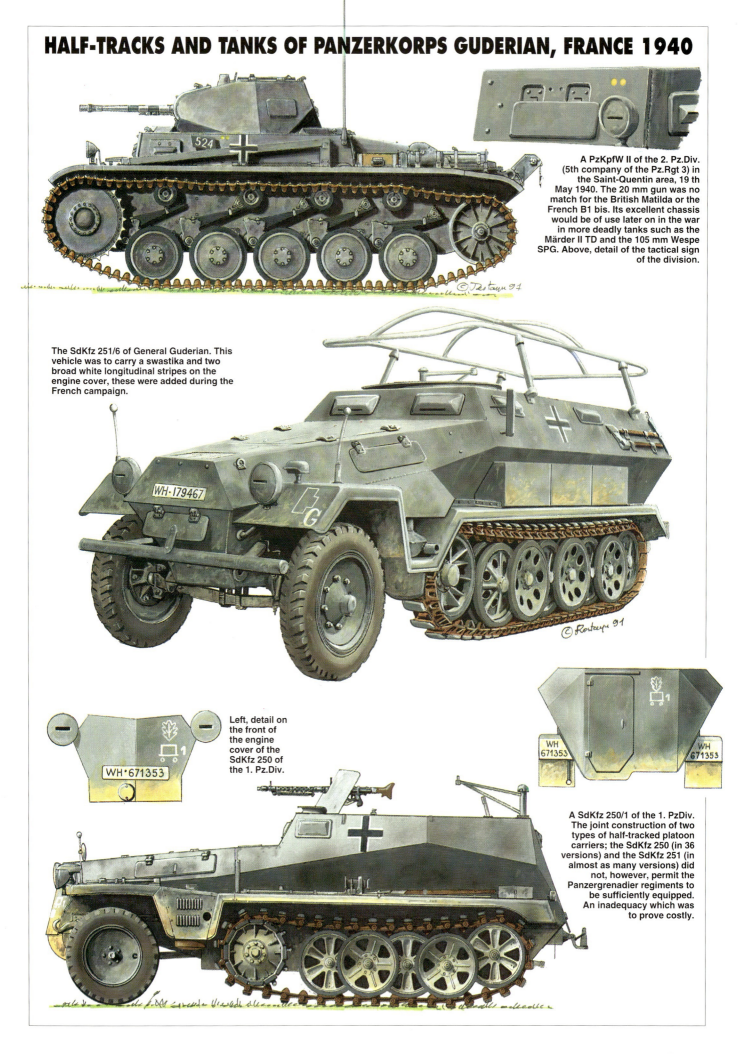

A PzKpfW II of the 2. Pz.Div. (5th company of the Pz.Rgt 3) in the Saint-Quentin area, 19 th May 1940. The 20 mm gun was no match for the British Matilda or the French B1 bis. Its excellent chassis would be of use later on in the war in more deadly tanks such as the Märder II TD and the 105 mm Wespe SPG. Above, detail of the tactical sign of the division.

The SdKfz 251/6 of General Guderian. This vehicle was to carry a swastika and two broad white longitudinal stripes on the engine cover, these were added during the French campaign.

Left, detail on the front of the engine cover of the SdKfz 250 of the 1. Pz.Div.

A SdKfz 250/1 of the 1. PzDiv. The joint construction of two types of half-tracked platoon carriers; the SdKfz 250 (in 36 versions) and the SdKfz 251 (in almost as many versions) did not, however, permit the Panzergrenadier regiments to be sufficiently equipped. An inadequacy which was to prove costly.

TANKS AND ASSAULT GUNS, DIVERSE UNITS, FRANCE 1940

A PzKpfW III (Panzerbefehlswagen III Ausführung E. SdKfz 266/267/268) command post of the 5th PzDiv.

Detail of the formation sign, painted close to the hull machine gun.

PzKpfW II (2cm) Ausf. B of the Pz.Rgt 9. S.Kp. of the 10 Panzer-Division.

Sturmgeschütz III Ausführung. A. of Sturmgeschütz-batterie 640, used under the command of the Infanterie-Regt 'Grossdeutschland', Stonne area. Only four batteries of StuG. III were used during the French campaign (in May 1940, a single battery was equipped with six assault guns). The success achieved by the StuG. III encouraged the Germans in their production of this AFV, feared because of its low outline and its excellent gun. The identification indicates the 2nd gun of the 1st Zug (2 guns per Zug and three Zugs per Battery).

THE PANZERKAMPFWAGEN 35 (t) SKODA, 1939-41

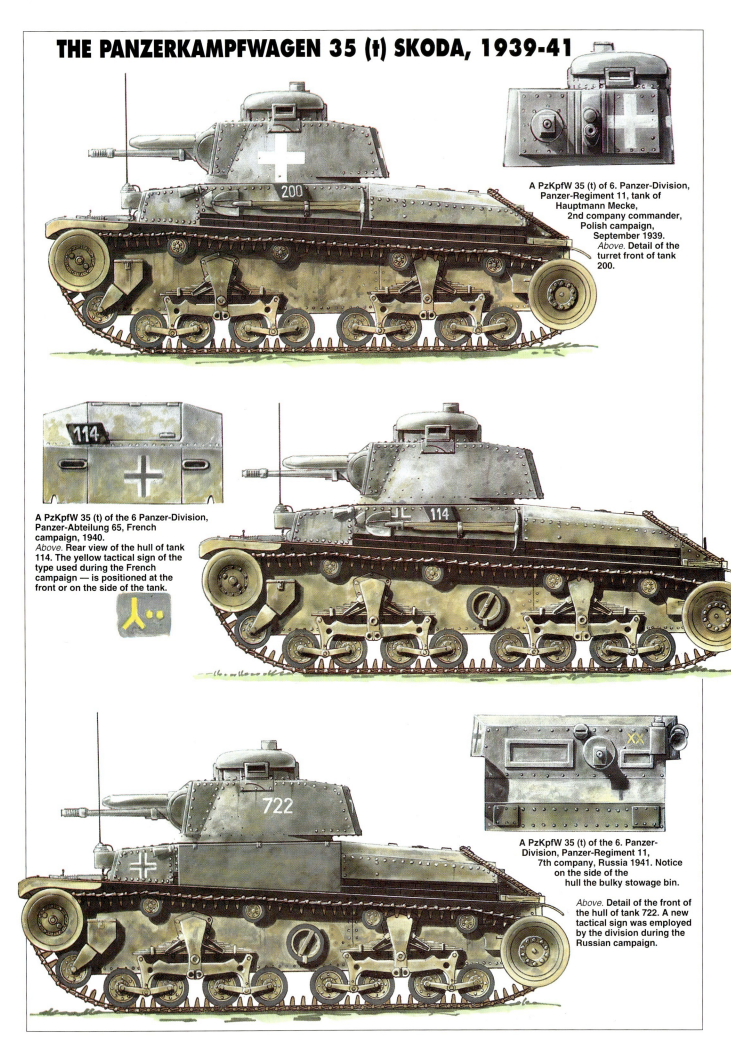

A PzKpfW 35 (t) of 6. Panzer-Division, Panzer-Regiment 11, tank of Hauptmann Mecke, 2nd company commander, Polish campaign, September 1939.
Above. Detail of the turret front of tank 200.

A PzKpfW 35 (t) of the 6 Panzer-Division, Panzer-Abteilung 65, French campaign, 1940.
Above. Rear view of the hull of tank 114. The yellow tactical sign of the type used during the French campaign — is positioned at the front or on the side of the tank.

A PzKpfW 35 (t) of the 6. Panzer-Division, Panzer-Regiment 11, 7th company, Russia 1941. Notice on the side of the hull the bulky stowage bin.

Above. Detail of the front of the hull of tank 722. A new tactical sign was employed by the division during the Russian campaign.

PANZERJÄGER I, 1940-41

Formation sign of *Panzerjäger-Abteilung 521*.

Above. **This Panzerjäger I belonged to** *Panzerabwehr-Abteilung 521*, which, from 2nd April 1940 was to become *Panzerjäger-Abteilung 521*. The insignia is positioned on each side of the vehicle. Later, the unit was to be equipped with more efficient tanks. At the beginning of the conflict the Panzerjäger I was the best tank destroyer and made the most efficient use of the Panzer I chassis.

Opposite. **Panzerjäger I of Panzerjäger-Abteilung 643.** This unit was to be transferred to *Panzer-Division "Gross Deutschland".* At that time the Stab and the 2nd company were incorporated in the *Panzerjäger- Abteilung GD*, whereas the 1st and 3rd companies were to be in the *Infanterie-Regiment GD Nº. 1.*

Below. **A Panzerjäger arriving in Tripoli in 1941. Like all German tanks of this period it is a Panzer grey colour; later the vehicles would be repainted in ochre or in a sand-coloured shade. This tank (1st vehicle, 1st battery) belonged to** *Panzerjäger Abteilung 605,* **an independent tank-destroyer unit.**

Opposite. **Panzerjäger-Abteilung 605's** sign. Once the tanks were repainted, the unit adopted a system of black figures on an olive green background.

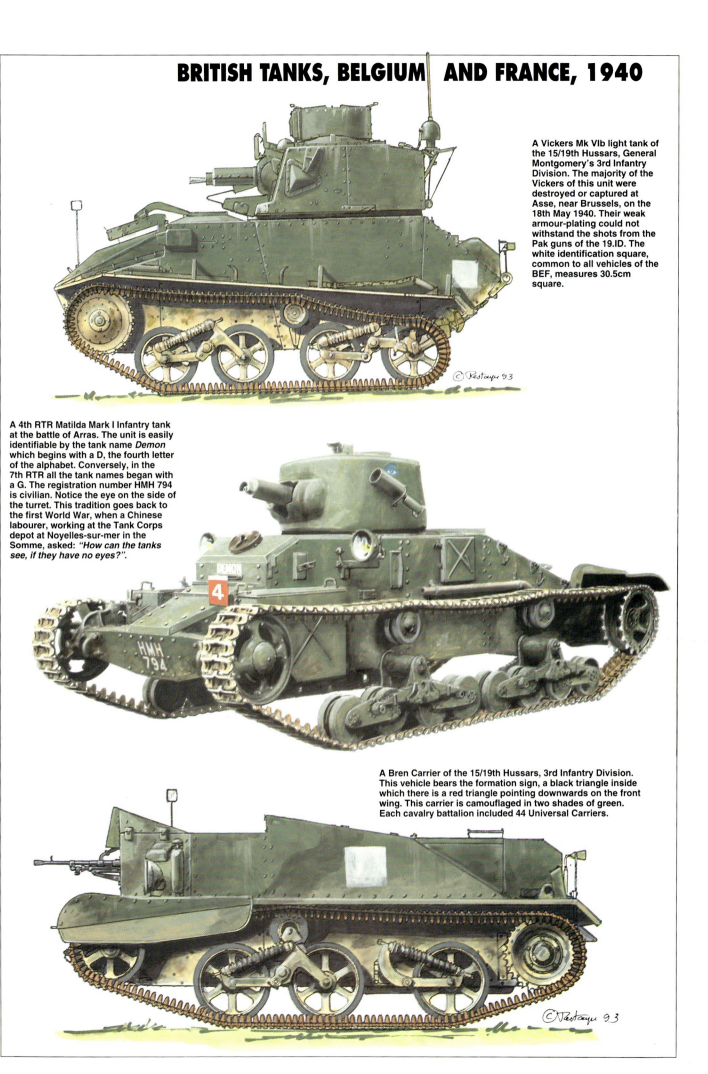

BRITISH TANKS, BELGIUM AND FRANCE, 1940

A Vickers Mk VIb light tank of the 15/19th Hussars, General Montgomery's 3rd Infantry Division. The majority of the Vickers of this unit were destroyed or captured at Asse, near Brussels, on the 18th May 1940. Their weak armour-plating could not withstand the shots from the Pak guns of the 19.ID. The white identification square, common to all vehicles of the BEF, measures 30.5cm square.

A 4th RTR Matilda Mark I Infantry tank at the battle of Arras. The unit is easily identifiable by the tank name *Demon* which begins with a D, the fourth letter of the alphabet. Conversely, in the 7th RTR all the tank names began with a G. The registration number HMH 794 is civilian. Notice the eye on the side of the turret. This tradition goes back to the first World War, when a Chinese labourer, working at the Tank Corps depot at Noyelles-sur-mer in the Somme, asked: *"How can the tanks see, if they have no eyes?"*.

A Bren Carrier of the 15/19th Hussars, 3rd Infantry Division. This vehicle bears the formation sign, a black triangle inside which there is a red triangle pointing downwards on the front wing. This carrier is camouflaged in two shades of green. Each cavalry battalion included 44 Universal Carriers.

INFANTRY TANKS OF THE BRITISH EXPEDITIONARY FORCE, 7th RTR

Matilda I of the 7th Royal Tank Regiment (C company). The camouflage is in two shades of green (G3/G4). Equipped with an excellent armour-plating, the Matilda I is armed only with a Vickers turret machine-gun. *"Glenlyon"* was to be abandoned by its 2-man crew after having been put out of combat in the Notre-Dame-de-Lorette region.

A Matilda II of the 7th RTR. A new conception compared with the Mark I, the *Infantry tank Mark II* was the most powerful British tank in 1940. Its thick armour was a major asset, counterbalanced by an inadequate 2 Pounder (40 mm) gun. The 7th RTR was the only unit equipped wit a Matilda IIs on the French front.

Another 7th RTR Matilda II. The badly-named *"Good Luck"* was to be destroyed by a direct hit on the front hull armour. The driver's hatches were torn out by the violence of the impact. In fact it was sheer luck for the German gunners as the armour of the Matilda withstood all German anti-tank guns, with the exception of the famous "88".

BELGIAN AND DUTCH AFVs, 1940

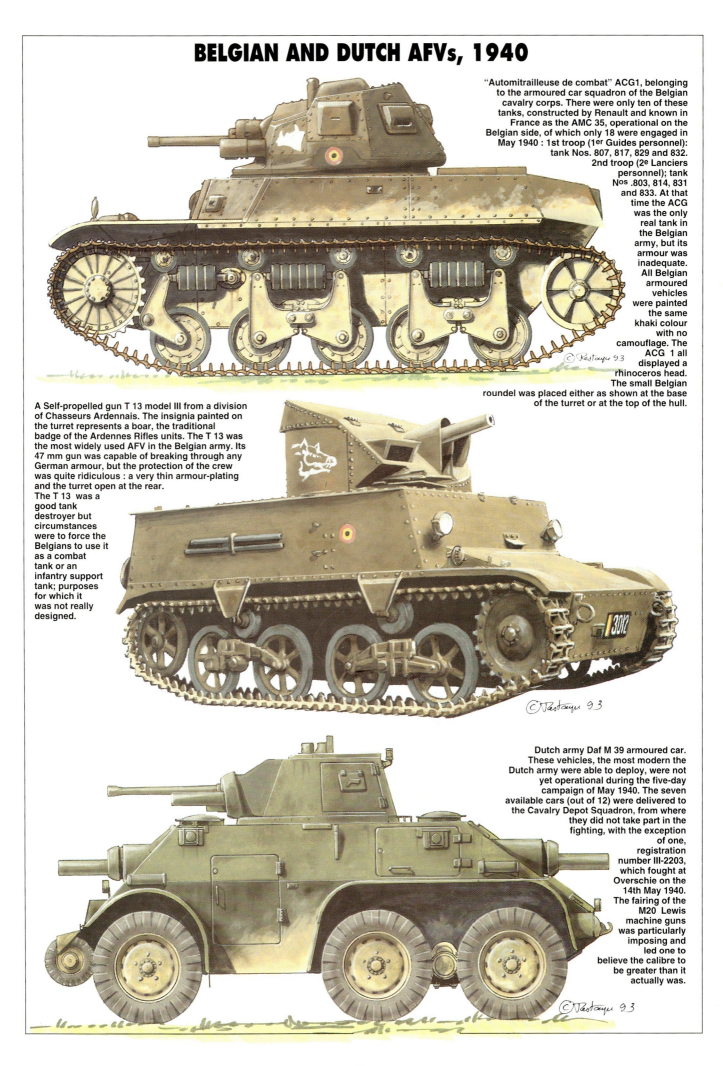

"Automitrailleuse de combat" ACG1, belonging to the armoured car squadron of the Belgian cavalry corps. There were only ten of these tanks, constructed by Renault and known in France as the AMC 35, operational on the Belgian side, of which only 18 were engaged in May 1940 : 1st troop (1er Guides personnel): tank Nos. 807, 817, 829 and 832. 2nd troop (2e Lanciers personnel); tank Nos .803, 814, 831 and 833. At that time the ACG was the only real tank in the Belgian army, but its armour was inadequate. All Belgian armoured vehicles were painted the same khaki colour with no camouflage. The ACG 1 all displayed a rhinoceros head. The small Belgian roundel was placed either as shown at the base of the turret or at the top of the hull.

A Self-propelled gun T 13 model III from a division of Chasseurs Ardennais. The insignia painted on the turret represents a boar, the traditional badge of the Ardennes Rifles units. The T 13 was the most widely used AFV in the Belgian army. Its 47 mm gun was capable of breaking through any German armour, but the protection of the crew was quite ridiculous : a very thin armour-plating and the turret open at the rear. The T 13 was a good tank destroyer but circumstances were to force the Belgians to use it as a combat tank or an infantry support tank; purposes for which it was not really designed.

Dutch army Daf M 39 armoured car. These vehicles, the most modern the Dutch army were able to deploy, were not yet operational during the five-day campaign of May 1940. The seven available cars (out of 12) were delivered to the Cavalry Depot Squadron, from where they did not take part in the fighting, with the exception of one, registration number III-2203, which fought at Overschie on the 14th May 1940. The fairing of the M20 Lewis machine guns was particularly imposing and led one to believe the calibre to be greater than it actually was.

FRENCH LAFFLY TANK DESTROYERS, MAY-JUNE 1940.

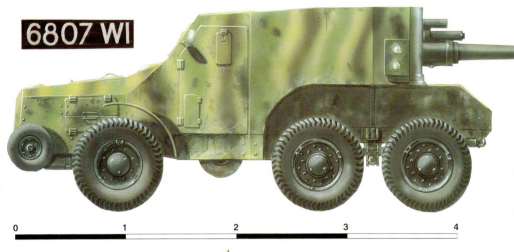

6807 WI

Armoured prototype of the Laffly W 15 TCC, March 1940. Several photos taken during this tank destroyer's trials show this rather distinctive camouflage, in broad stripes, the exact shades of which cannot be established with certainty. The wheels were certainly painted in black, as was the case on many French vehicles of the period. The 'W' registration numbers are attributed to the makers for the temporary registration of their vehicles.

0 1 2 3 4

A standard Laffly W 15 TCC. Directly inspired from a factory shot, this three-quarter rear view of vehicle P 17 079 (Nº. 3 of its platoon) emphasises the 47 mm AC 1937 model gun. The standard shield is complete with additional armour-plating. The production Laffly TDs were systematically camouflaged in the factory in two matt shades. The colours we have used, olive green (background) and chocolate brown (blotches), are consistent with the period French rules and the time of the year. Nevertheless, we give them without assurance.

A Laffly W 15 TCC, Nº. 5 of its platoon. We have represented it here with its 24/29 LMG on one of the two AA mounts. The military registration conforms with the regulation of the period : a continuous series of five figures preceded by the French tricolour. To the left is the letter M (vehicles produced from 1938 to the beginning of 1940), then the letter P for the most recent. Vehicles produced before the 'M' series was introduced had no letter at all.

P 17 076

Front view of an armoured windscreen with the French roundel.

LIGHT TANK MODEL 1935 R (Renault R 35)

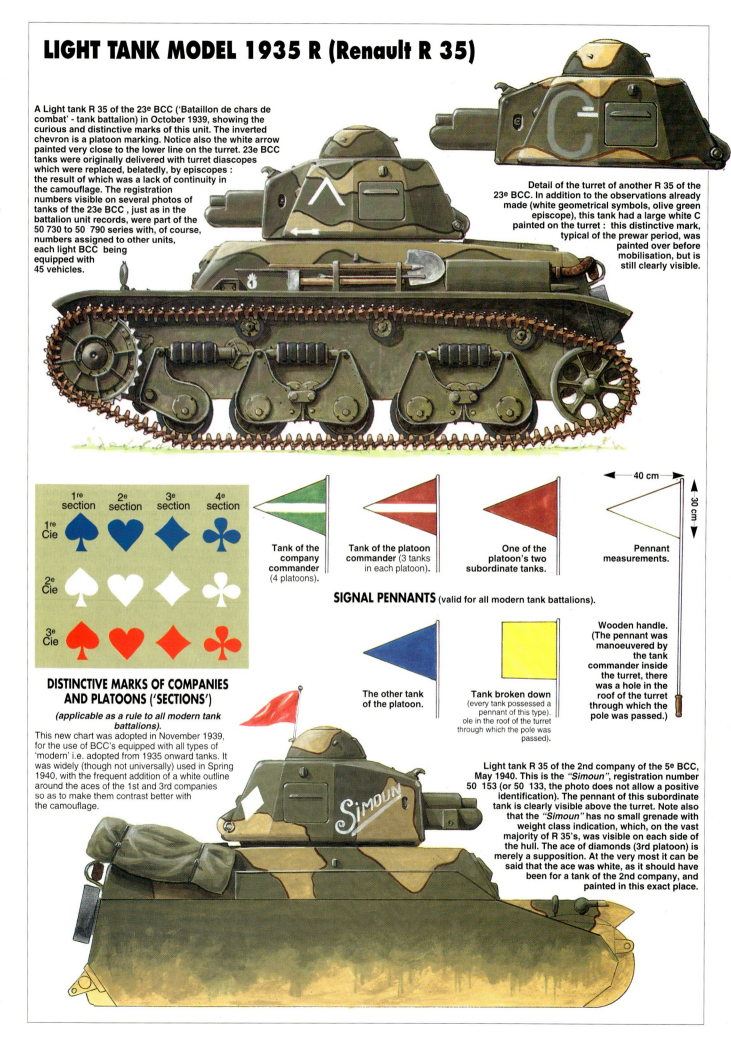

A Light tank R 35 of the 23e BCC ('Bataillon de chars de combat' - tank battalion) in October 1939, showing the curious and distinctive marks of this unit. The inverted chevron is a platoon marking. Notice also the white arrow painted very close to the lower line on the turret. 23e BCC tanks were originally delivered with turret diascopes which were replaced, belatedly, by episcopes : the result of which was a lack of continuity in the camouflage. The registration numbers visible on several photos of tanks of the 23e BCC , just as in the battalion unit records, were part of the 50 730 to 50 790 series with, of course, numbers assigned to other units, each light BCC being equipped with 45 vehicles.

Detail of the turret of another R 35 of the 23e BCC. In addition to the observations already made (white geometrical symbols, olive green episcope), this tank had a large white C painted on the turret : this distinctive mark, typical of the prewar period, was painted over before mobilisation, but is still clearly visible.

	1re section	2e section	3e section	4e section
1re Cie	♠	♥	♦	♣
2e Cie	♠	♥	♦	♣
3e Cie	♠	♥	♦	♣

Tank of the company commander (4 platoons).

Tank of the platoon commander (3 tanks in each platoon).

One of the platoon's two subordinate tanks.

Pennant measurements.

← 40 cm →

30 cm

SIGNAL PENNANTS (valid for all modern tank battalions).

The other tank of the platoon.

Tank broken down (every tank possessed a pennant of this type). ole in the roof of the turret through which the pole was passed).

Wooden handle. (The pennant was manoeuvered by the tank commander inside the turret, there was a hole in the roof of the turret through which the pole was passed.)

DISTINCTIVE MARKS OF COMPANIES AND PLATOONS ('SECTIONS')

(applicable as a rule to all modern tank battalions).

This new chart was adopted in November 1939, for the use of BCC's equipped with all types of 'modern' i.e. adopted from 1935 onward tanks. It was widely (though not universally) used in Spring 1940, with the frequent addition of a white outline around the aces of the 1st and 3rd companies so as to make them contrast better with the camouflage.

Light tank R 35 of the 2nd company of the 5e BCC, May 1940. This is the *"Simoun"*, registration number 50 153 (or 50 133, the photo does not allow a positive identification). The pennant of this subordinate tank is clearly visible above the turret. Note also that the *"Simoun"* has no small grenade with weight class indication, which, on the vast majority of R 35's, was visible on each side of the hull. The ace of diamonds (3rd platoon) is merely a supposition. At the very most it can be said that the ace was white, as it should have been for a tank of the 2nd company, and painted in this exact place.

1935 R MODEL LIGHT TANK (Renault R 35)

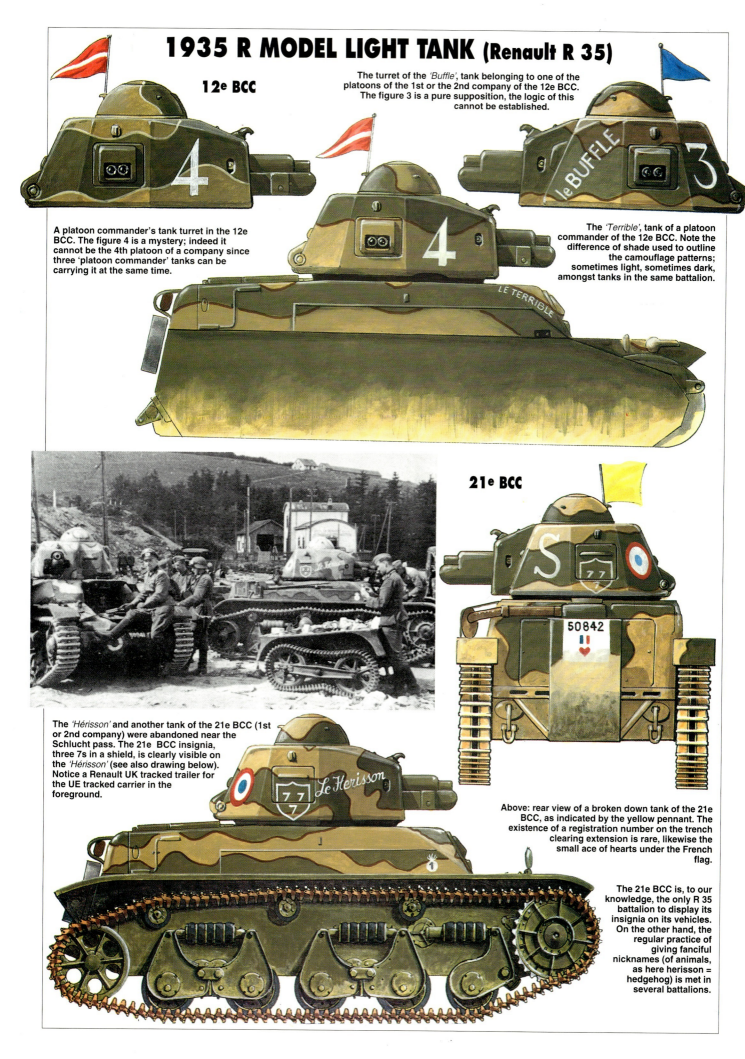

12e BCC

The turret of the 'Buffle', tank belonging to one of the platoons of the 1st or the 2nd company of the 12e BCC. The figure 3 is a pure supposition, the logic of this cannot be established.

A platoon commander's tank turret in the 12e BCC. The figure 4 is a mystery; indeed it cannot be the 4th platoon of a company since three 'platoon commander' tanks can be carrying it at the same time.

The 'Terrible', tank of a platoon commander of the 12e BCC. Note the difference of shade used to outline the camouflage patterns; sometimes light, sometimes dark, amongst tanks in the same battalion.

21e BCC

The 'Hérisson' and another tank of the 21e BCC (1st or 2nd company) were abandoned near the Schlucht pass. The 21e BCC insignia, three 7s in a shield, is clearly visible on the 'Hérisson' (see also drawing below). Notice a Renault UK tracked trailer for the UE tracked carrier in the foreground.

Above: rear view of a broken down tank of the 21e BCC, as indicated by the yellow pennant. The existence of a registration number on the trench clearing extension is rare, likewise the small ace of hearts under the French flag.

The 21e BCC is, to our knowledge, the only R 35 battalion to display its insignia on its vehicles. On the other hand, the regular practice of giving fanciful nicknames (of animals, as here herisson = hedgehog) is met in several battalions.

RENAULT R 40 LIGHT TANK (1940 MODIFIED 1935 R MODEL)

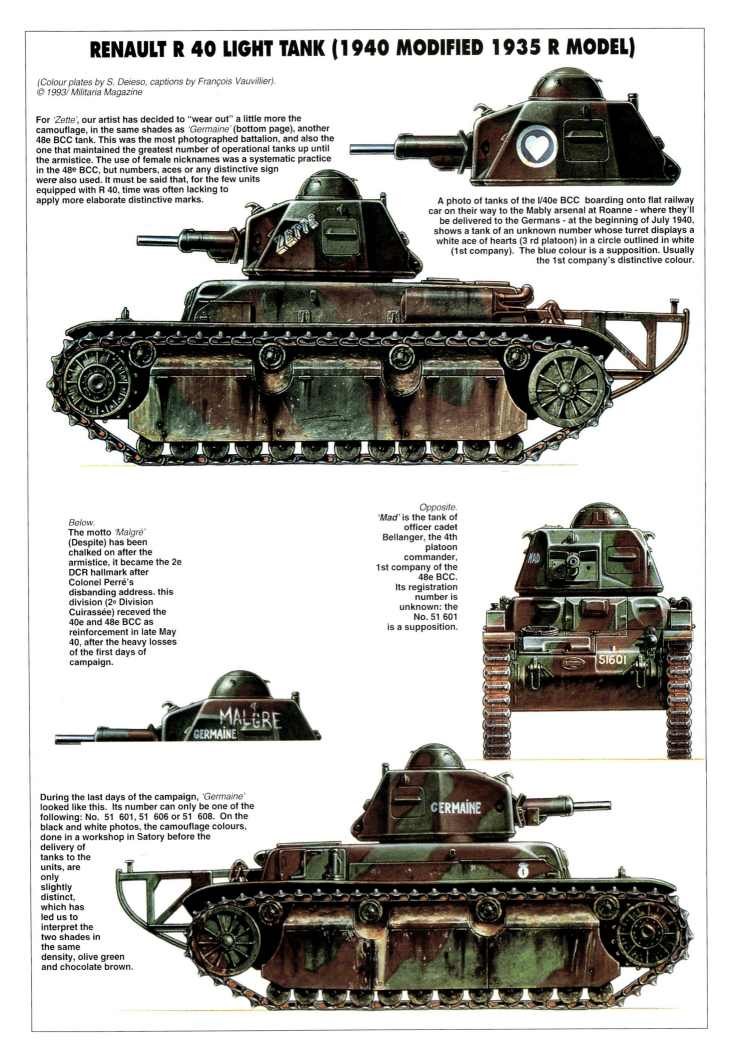

(Colour plates by S. Deieso, captions by François Vauvillier).
© 1993/ Militaria Magazine

For *'Zette'*, our artist has decided to "wear out" a little more the camouflage, in the same shades as *'Germaine'* (bottom page), another 48e BCC tank. This was the most photographed battalion, and also the one that maintained the greatest number of operational tanks up until the armistice. The use of female nicknames was a systematic practice in the 48e BCC, but numbers, aces or any distinctive sign were also used. It must be said that, for the few units equipped with R 40, time was often lacking to apply more elaborate distinctive marks.

A photo of tanks of the I/40e BCC boarding onto flat railway car on their way to the Mably arsenal at Roanne - where they'll be delivered to the Germans - at the beginning of July 1940, shows a tank of an unknown number whose turret displays a white ace of hearts (3 rd platoon) in a circle outlined in white (1st company). The blue colour is a supposition. Usually the 1st company's distinctive colour.

Below.
The motto *'Malgré'* (Despite) has been chalked on after the armistice, it became the 2e DCR hallmark after Colonel Perré's disbanding address. this division (2e Division Cuirassée) receved the 40e and 48e BCC as reinforcement in late May 40, after the heavy losses of the first days of campaign.

Opposite.
'Mad' is the tank of officer cadet Bellanger, the 4th platoon commander, 1st company of the 48e BCC. Its registration number is unknown: the No. 51 601 is a supposition.

During the last days of the campaign, *'Germaine'* looked like this. Its number can only be one of the following: No. 51 601, 51 606 or 51 608. On the black and white photos, the camouflage colours, done in a workshop in Satory before the delivery of tanks to the units, are only slightly distinct, which has led us to interpret the two shades in the same density, olive green and chocolate brown.

THE FIRST FRENCH AFVs ENGAGED IN THE ARDENNES

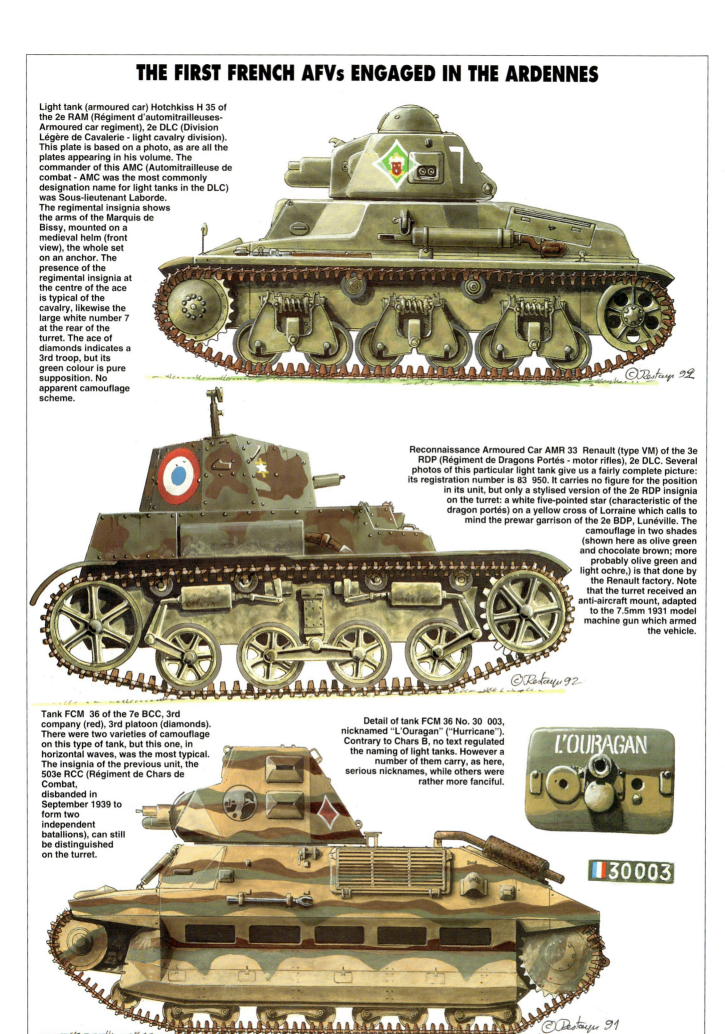

Light tank (armoured car) Hotchkiss H 35 of the 2e RAM (Régiment d'automitrailleuses-Armoured car regiment), 2e DLC (Division Légère de Cavalerie - light cavalry division). This plate is based on a photo, as are all the plates appearing in his volume. The commander of this AMC (Automitrailleuse de combat - AMC was the most commonly designation name for light tanks in the DLC) was Sous-lieutenant Laborde. The regimental insignia shows the arms of the Marquis de Bissy, mounted on a medieval helm (front view), the whole set on an anchor. The presence of the regimental insignia at the centre of the ace is typical of the cavalry, likewise the large white number 7 at the rear of the turret. The ace of diamonds indicates a 3rd troop, but its green colour is pure supposition. No apparent camouflage scheme.

Reconnaissance Armoured Car AMR 33 Renault (type VM) of the 3e RDP (Régiment de Dragons Portés - motor rifles), 2e DLC. Several photos of this particular light tank give us a fairly complete picture: its registration number is 83 950. It carries no figure for the position in its unit, but only a stylised version of the 2e RDP insignia on the turret: a white five-pointed star (characteristic of the dragon portés) on a yellow cross of Lorraine which calls to mind the prewar garrison of the 2e BDP, Lunéville. The camouflage in two shades (shown here as olive green and chocolate brown; more probably olive green and light ochre,) is that done by the Renault factory. Note that the turret received an anti-aircraft mount, adapted to the 7.5mm 1931 model machine gun which armed the vehicle.

Tank FCM 36 of the 7e BCC, 3rd company (red), 3rd platoon (diamonds). There were two varieties of camouflage on this type of tank, but this one, in horizontal waves, was the most typical. The insignia of the previous unit, the 503e RCC (Régiment de Chars de Combat, disbanded in September 1939 to form two independent batallions), can still be distinguished on the turret.

Detail of tank FCM 36 No. 30 003, nicknamed "L'Ouragan" ("Hurricane"). Contrary to Chars B, no text regulated the naming of light tanks. However a number of them carry, as here, serious nicknames, while others were rather more fanciful.

FRENCH AFVs

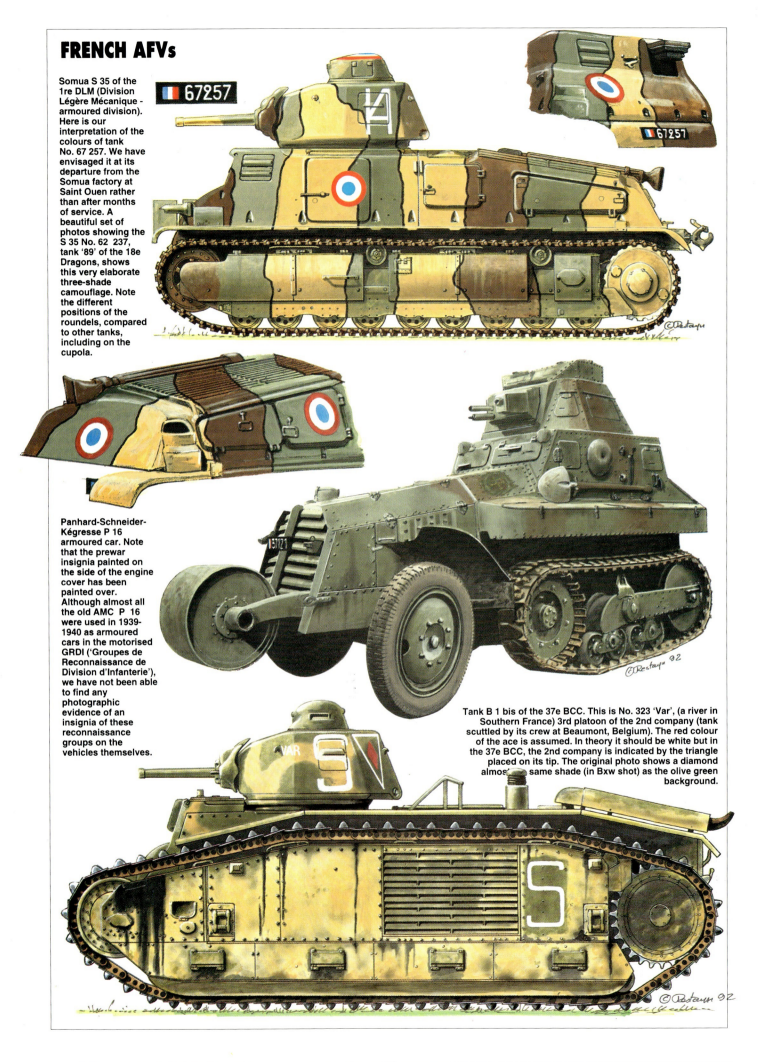

Somua S 35 of the 1re DLM (Division Légère Mécanique - armoured division). Here is our interpretation of the colours of tank No. 67 257. We have envisaged it at its departure from the Somua factory at Saint Ouen rather than after months of service. A beautiful set of photos showing the S 35 No. 62 237, tank '89' of the 18e Dragons, shows this very elaborate three-shade camouflage. Note the different positions of the roundels, compared to other tanks, including on the cupola.

67257

Panhard-Schneider-Kégresse P 16 armoured car. Note that the prewar insignia painted on the side of the engine cover has been painted over. Although almost all the old AMC P 16 were used in 1939-1940 as armoured cars in the motorised GRDI ('Groupes de Reconnaissance de Division d'Infanterie'), we have not been able to find any photographic evidence of an insignia of these reconnaissance groups on the vehicles themselves.

Tank B 1 bis of the 37e BCC. This is No. 323 'Var', (a river in Southern France) 3rd platoon of the 2nd company (tank scuttled by its crew at Beaumont, Belgium). The red colour of the ace is assumed. In theory it should be white but in the 37e BCC, the 2nd company is indicated by the triangle placed on its tip. The original photo shows a diamond almost the same shade (in Bxw shot) as the olive green background.

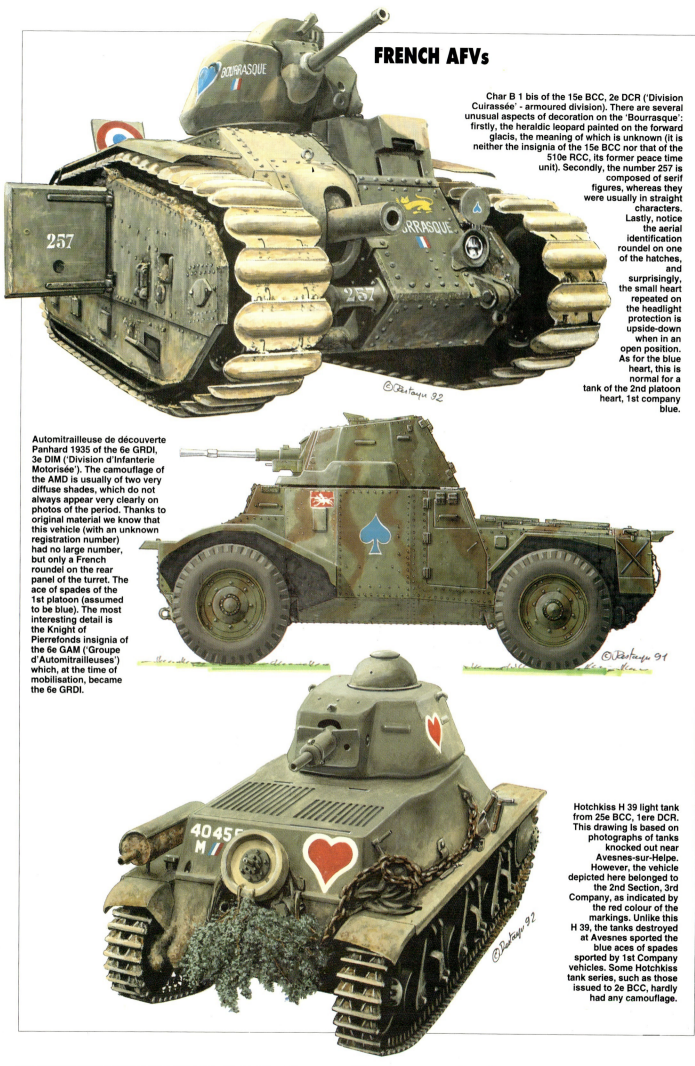

FRENCH AFVs

Char B 1 bis of the 15e BCC, 2e DCR ('Division Cuirassée' - armoured division). There are several unusual aspects of decoration on the 'Bourrasque': firstly, the heraldic leopard painted on the forward glacis, the meaning of which is unknown (it is neither the insignia of the 15e BCC nor that of the 510e RCC, its former peace time unit). Secondly, the number 257 is composed of serif figures, whereas they were usually in straight characters. Lastly, notice the aerial identification roundel on one of the hatches, and surprisingly, the small heart repeated on the headlight protection is upside-down when in an open position. As for the blue heart, this is normal for a tank of the 2nd platoon heart, 1st company blue.

Automitrailleuse de découverte Panhard 1935 of the 6e GRDI, 3e DIM ('Division d'Infanterie Motorisée'). The camouflage of the AMD is usually of two very diffuse shades, which do not always appear very clearly on photos of the period. Thanks to original material we know that this vehicle (with an unknown registration number) had no large number, but only a French roundel on the rear panel of the turret. The ace of spades of the 1st platoon (assumed to be blue). The most interesting detail is the Knight of Pierrefonds insignia of the 6e GAM ('Groupe d'Automitrailleuses') which, at the time of mobilisation, became the 6e GRDI.

Hotchkiss H 39 light tank from 25e BCC, 1ere DCR. This drawing is based on photographs of tanks knocked out near Avesnes-sur-Helpe. However, the vehicle depicted here belonged to the 2nd Section, 3rd Company, as indicated by the red colour of the markings. Unlike this H 39, the tanks destroyed at Avesnes sported the blue aces of spades sported by 1st Company vehicles. Some Hotchkiss tank series, such as those issued to 2e BCC, hardly had any camouflage.

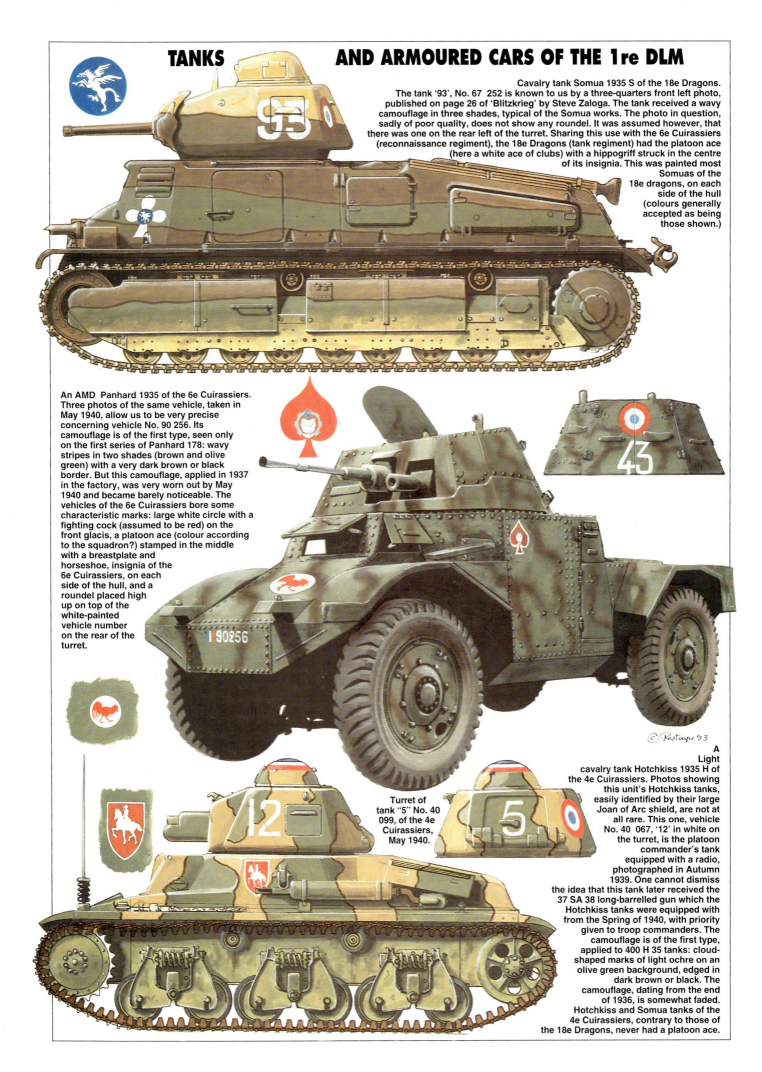

Cavalry tank Somua 1935 S of the 18e Dragons. The tank '93', No. 67 252 is known to us by a three-quarters front left photo, published on page 26 of 'Blitzkrieg' by Steve Zaloga. The tank received a wavy camouflage in three shades, typical of the Somua works. The photo in question, sadly of poor quality, does not show any roundel. It was assumed however, that there was one on the rear left of the turret. Sharing this use with the 6e Cuirassiers (reconnaissance regiment), the 18e Dragons (tank regiment) had the platoon ace (here a white ace of clubs) with a hippogriff struck in the centre of its insignia. This was painted most Somuas of the 18e dragons, on each side of the hull (colours generally accepted as being those shown.)

An AMD Panhard 1935 of the 6e Cuirassiers. Three photos of the same vehicle, taken in May 1940, allow us to be very precise concerning vehicle No. 90 256. Its camouflage is of the first type, seen only on the first series of Panhard 178: wavy stripes in two shades (brown and olive green) with a very dark brown or black border. But this camouflage, applied in 1937 in the factory, was very worn out by May 1940 and became barely noticeable. The vehicles of the 6e Cuirassiers bore some characteristic marks: large white circle with a fighting cock (assumed to be red) on the front glacis, a platoon ace (colour according to the squadron?) stamped in the middle with a breastplate and horseshoe, insignia of the 6e Cuirassiers, on each side of the hull, and a roundel placed high up on top of the white-painted vehicle number on the rear of the turret.

Turret of tank "5" No. 40 099, of the 4e Cuirassiers, May 1940.

A Light cavalry tank Hotchkiss 1935 H of the 4e Cuirassiers. Photos showing this unit's Hotchkiss tanks, easily identified by their large Joan of Arc shield, are not at all rare. This one, vehicle No. 40 067, '12' in white on the turret, is the platoon commander's tank equipped with a radio, photographed in Autumn 1939. One cannot dismiss the idea that this tank later received the 37 SA 38 long-barrelled gun which the Hotchkiss tanks were equipped with from the Spring of 1940, with priority given to troop commanders. The camouflage is of the first type, applied to 400 H 35 tanks: cloud-shaped marks of light ochre on an olive green background, edged in dark brown or black. The camouflage, dating from the end of 1936, is somewhat faded. Hotchkiss and Somua tanks of the 4e Cuirassiers, contrary to those of the 18e Dragons, never had a platoon ace.

© Restayn 93

CAVALRY TANKS AND ARMOURED CARS OF THE 2e DLM

A cavalry tank Somua 1935 S of the 29e Dragons. This tank, registration number M 914, was abandoned near Crevecoeur-sur-Escaut at the end of May 1940. The Somua of the 2e DLM are readily recognisable by the presence of small aces at the front of the turret, added to the usual large white figures painted at the rear. A less absolute identification sign was the fact that the tanks belonged to the 22300 registration series or to the M 800/900 series, the latter was shared with the 1re DLM. Their camouflage is the horizontal line type, but on the M 800/900 series the edges were bordered in a dark shade. In the DLM, the distinction between the two combat regiments is made (apart from possible regimental insignia) by a series of white numbers on the turret: under 50 for the first regiment (13e Dragons) and above 50 for the second (29e Dragons). On the tank '83' here, the 3 is visible on the wartime photo but the 8 is an assumption as it is almost indiscernible. The most striking element of tank M 914 is the small circular insignia on the access hatch which is a stylised version of the Tower of Provins, insignia of the 29e Dragons, seen repeatedly on Somua tanks of this regiment. The tank bears two roundels: one on the cupola and another (not visible here) on the turret rear door.

Back of turret of AMR 35 '2' No. 87 368, of the 1er RDP, April 1938.

Reconnaissance Armoured Car AMR 35 Renault (type ZT) of the 1er Régiment de Dragons Portés. Here, AMR No. 87 403 was part of a batch armed with a 13.2mm machine gun, which was taken during a parade at the Bossut quarters in Pontoise just before the war. Two-shade camouflage with black, merged-in, edges. A small roundel on the turret, the ace of spades of the troop on the hull. On the turret a small white circle is discernible, just after the roundel, with no doubt a pattern inside.

The tactical sign (a diamond, top-half colour indicating the battalion: dark blue for the 1st battalion, red for the 2nd, and green for the 3rd, the bottom half indicating the squadron, dark blue for the armoured car squadron), as regulated by unit instructions in the 1er RDP on 29th September 1939, is painted on the rear right stowage bin. It may also be seen on a photo published on page 215 of 'May 1940' by Peter Taghon. The figure indicates the platoon.

Light cavalry tank Hotchkiss 1935 H assumed to be from the 29e Dragons. 'The Bison', tank '50' No. 40 228, is known to us by an unpublished German photo. It is a troop commander's tank, with a radio mount (the aerial is missing), rearmed with a 37mm SA 38 long-barrelled gun. Its camouflage was that common to all the H 35s. Here again the ace on the hull (colour unknown) at the same time as a white number, signifies membership of the 2e DLM (although this system is also used on the 18e Dragons' Hotchkiss tanks, belonging to the 1re DLM!). But no doubt remains as the small white Cross of Lorraine (very rarely seen on the tanks, however), adopted by General René Altmayer for his division the 2e DLM in September 1939 is clearly visible on the hull side.

CAVALRY TANKS AND ARMOURED CARS OF THE 3e DLM

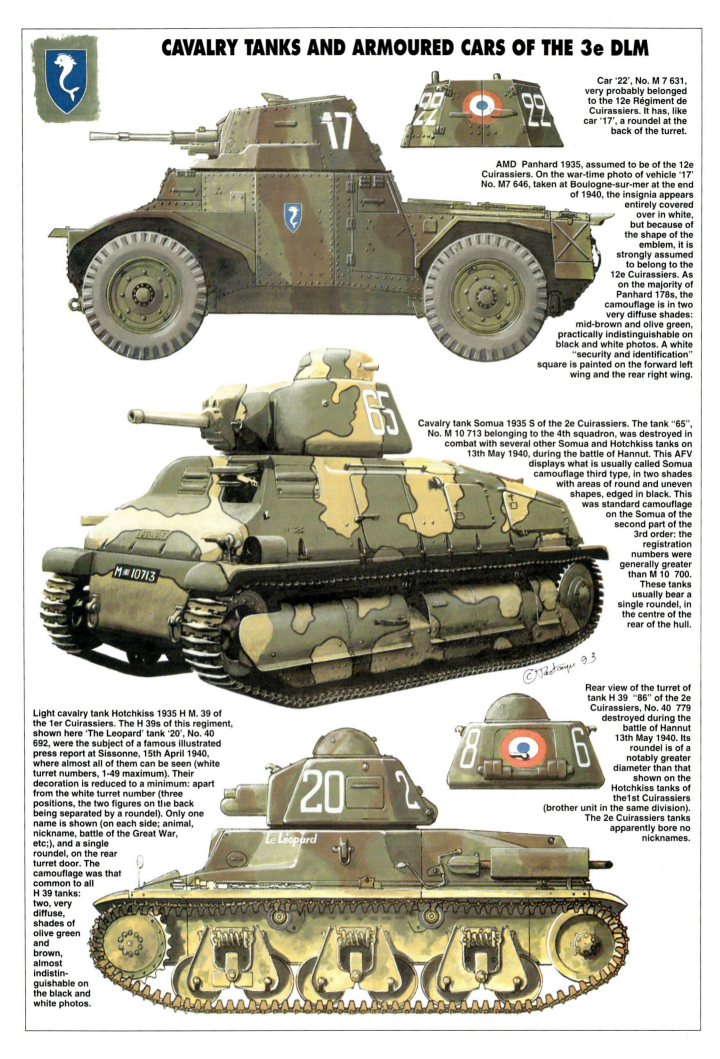

Car '22', No. M 7 631, very probably belonged to the 12e Régiment de Cuirassiers. It has, like car '17', a roundel at the back of the turret.

AMD Panhard 1935, assumed to be of the 12e Cuirassiers. On the war-time photo of vehicle '17' No. M7 646, taken at Boulogne-sur-mer at the end of 1940, the insignia appears entirely covered over in white, but because of the shape of the emblem, it is strongly assumed to belong to the 12e Cuirassiers. As on the majority of Panhard 178s, the camouflage is in two very diffuse shades: mid-brown and olive green, practically indistinguishable on black and white photos. A white "security and identification" square is painted on the forward left wing and the rear right wing.

Cavalry tank Somua 1935 S of the 2e Cuirassiers. The tank "65", No. M 10 713 belonging to the 4th squadron, was destroyed in combat with several other Somua and Hotchkiss tanks on 13th May 1940, during the battle of Hannut. This AFV displays what is usually called Somua camouflage third type, in two shades with areas of round and uneven shapes, edged in black. This was standard camouflage on the Somua of the second part of the 3rd order: the registration numbers were generally greater than M 10 700. These tanks usually bear a single roundel, in the centre of the rear of the hull.

Light cavalry tank Hotchkiss 1935 H M. 39 of the 1er Cuirassiers. The H 39s of this regiment, shown here 'The Leopard' tank '20', No. 40 692, were the subject of a famous illustrated press report at Sissonne, 15th April 1940, where almost all of them can be seen (white turret numbers, 1-49 maximum). Their decoration is reduced to a minimum: apart from the white turret number (three positions, the two figures on the back being separated by a roundel). Only one name is shown (on each side; animal, nickname, battle of the Great War, etc;), and a single roundel, on the rear turret door. The camouflage was that common to all H 39 tanks: two, very diffuse, shades of olive green and brown, almost indistinguishable on the black and white photos.

Rear view of the turret of tank H 39 "86" of the 2e Cuirassiers, No. 40 779 destroyed during the battle of Hannut 13th May 1940. Its roundel is of a notably greater diameter than that shown on the Hotchkiss tanks of the1st Cuirassiers (brother unit in the same division). The 2e Cuirassiers tanks apparently bore no nicknames.

1940
WAR IN
THE DESERT

ITALIAN AFVS, IN THE DESERT, 1940-1941

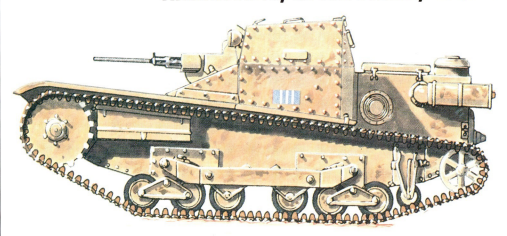

Carro Veloce L 3/33 or CV 33 bearing the tactical mark of a 3rd troop of a 2nd company, probably of the Trento division, in summer 1940. This AFV, which was nothing more than an armed carrier with no real value as a fighting vehicle, was used by the majority of Italian armoured battalions.

Autoblinda AB 40/41 armed with a 20mm gun. The Italian forces did not use this excellent armoured car to its full potential; it was mostly used as an escort vehicle or for the transport of senior officers. But the British and the Germans knew how to get the best from the Autoblinda used in their ranks. The British encountered them as war booty and the Germans as loan vehicles.

Fiat-Ansaldo M 11/39 medium tank, unit unknown, perhaps the Littorio armoured division. This tank was a failure on all points; feebly armed with thin armour, the tank commander and the gun-loader were positioned on different levels with no possibility of communicating. To want to attack a Matilda in such a tank was tantamount to suicide. During the Africa campaign, the Italian troops lacked good equipment rather than courage.

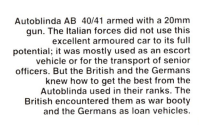

0   1   2   3   4

ITALIAN AFVs OF THE ARIETE DIVISION

This tank without a turret is a Carro comando M 40 of the 132nd Ariete armoured division, in Cyrenaica, January 1942. These AFVs were used as command posts in the units equipped with Semovente assault guns.

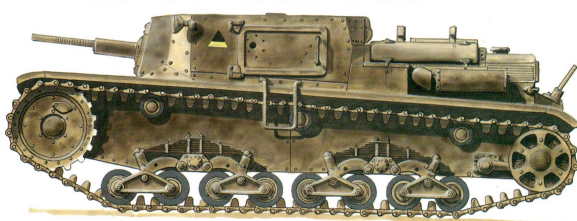

A Camionetta Desertica AS 37. This excellent car, very much appreciated by all the belligerents, was still constructed after the war on the basis of the Carro Protetto AS 37.

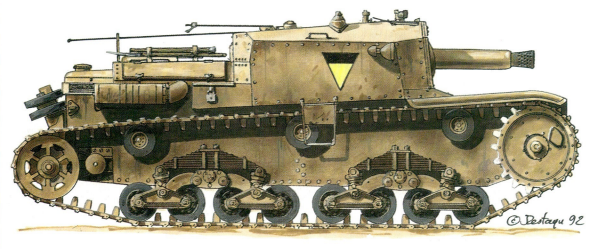

Below: Details of the forward and rear sides of the Semovente.

A Semovente M 40 da 75/18, beginning of 1942, Cyrenaica. This assault gun belonged to the 132nd Ariete armoured division. Its 75mm gun meant that, in January 1942, the Semovente possessed an unequalled fire power.

THE ITALIAN M 13/40 TANK

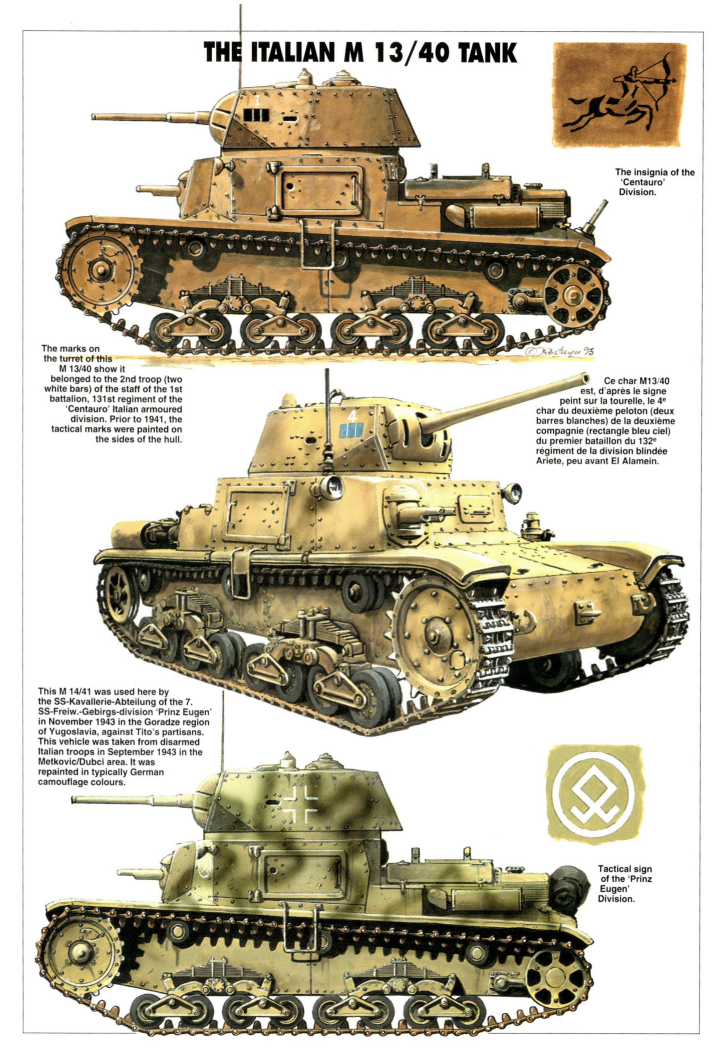

The insignia of the 'Centauro' Division.

The marks on the turret of this M 13/40 show it belonged to the 2nd troop (two white bars) of the staff of the 1st battalion, 131st regiment of the 'Centauro' Italian armoured division. Prior to 1941, the tactical marks were painted on the sides of the hull.

Ce char M13/40 est, d'après le signe peint sur la tourelle, le 4e char du deuxième peloton (deux barres blanches) de la deuxième compagnie (rectangle bleu ciel) du premier bataillon du 132e régiment de la division blindée Ariete, peu avant El Alamein.

This M 14/41 was used here by the SS-Kavallerie-Abteilung of the 7. SS-Freiw.-Gebirgs-division 'Prinz Eugen' in November 1943 in the Goradze region of Yugoslavia, against Tito's partisans. This vehicle was taken from disarmed Italian troops in September 1943 in the Metkovic/Dubci area. It was repainted in typically German camouflage colours.

Tactical sign of the 'Prinz Eugen' Division.

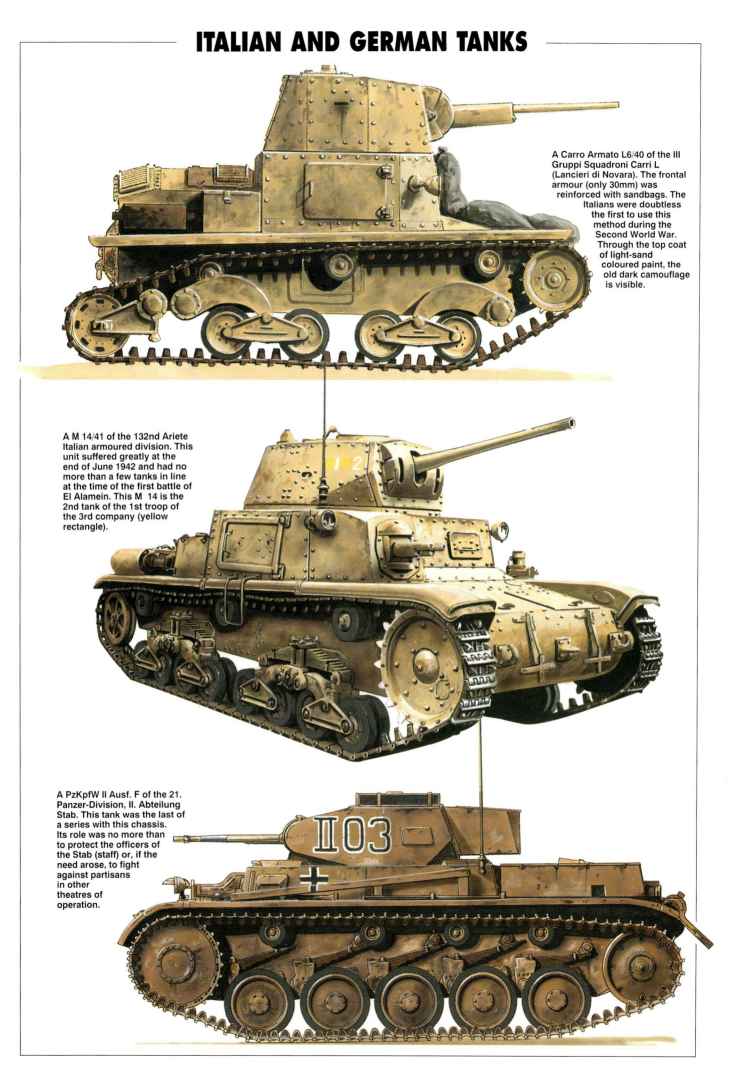

A Carro Armato L6/40 of the III Gruppi Squadroni Carri L (Lancieri di Novara). The frontal armour (only 30mm) was reinforced with sandbags. The Italians were doubtless the first to use this method during the Second World War. Through the top coat of light-sand coloured paint, the old dark camouflage is visible.

A M 14/41 of the 132nd Ariete Italian armoured division. This unit suffered greatly at the end of June 1942 and had no more than a few tanks in line at the time of the first battle of El Alamein. This M 14 is the 2nd tank of the 1st troop of the 3rd company (yellow rectangle).

A PzKpfW II Ausf. F of the 21. Panzer-Division, II. Abteilung Stab. This tank was the last of a series with this chassis. Its role was no more than to protect the officers of the Stab (staff) or, if the need arose, to fight against partisans in other theatres of operation.

LIGHT AFVs OF THE DEUTSCHER AFRIKAKORPS

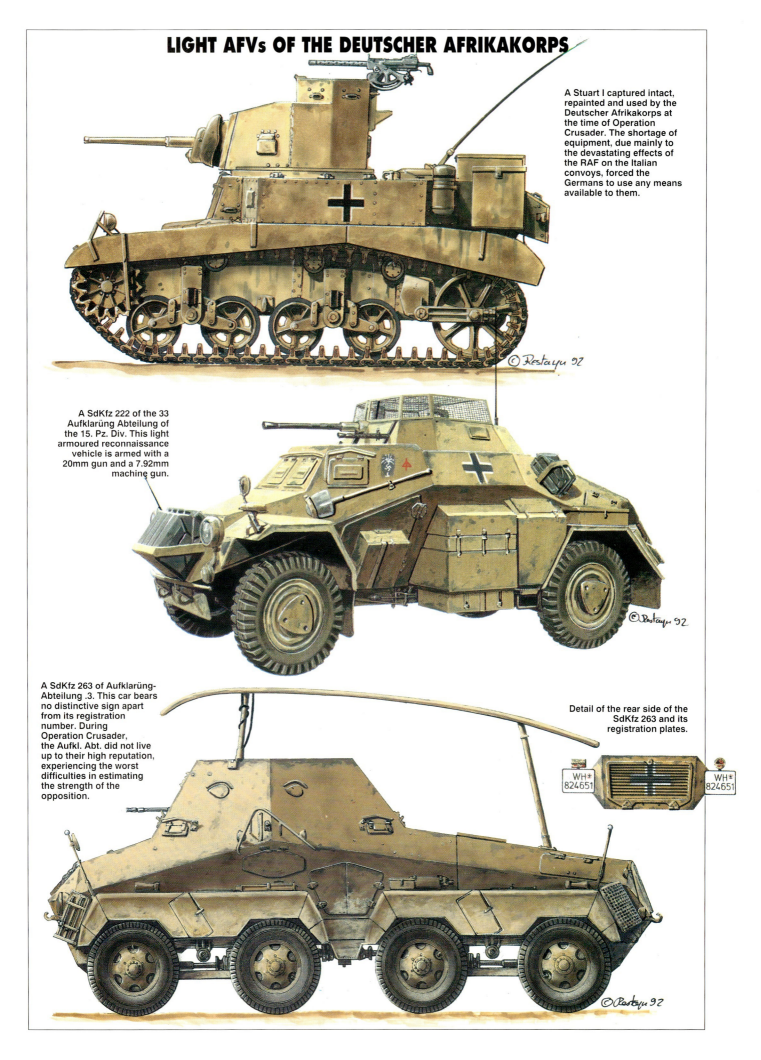

A Stuart I captured intact, repainted and used by the Deutscher Afrikakorps at the time of Operation Crusader. The shortage of equipment, due mainly to the devastating effects of the RAF on the Italian convoys, forced the Germans to use any means available to them.

A SdKfz 222 of the 33 Aufklarüng Abteilung of the 15. Pz. Div. This light armoured reconnaissance vehicle is armed with a 20mm gun and a 7.92mm machine gun.

A SdKfz 263 of Aufklarüng-Abteilung .3. This car bears no distinctive sign apart from its registration number. During Operation Crusader, the Aufkl. Abt. did not live up to their high reputation, experiencing the worst difficulties in estimating the strength of the opposition.

Detail of the rear side of the SdKfz 263 and its registration plates.

WH* 824651

WH* 824651

© Restayn 92

© Restayn 92

© Restayn 92

LIGHT AND MEDIUM TANKS

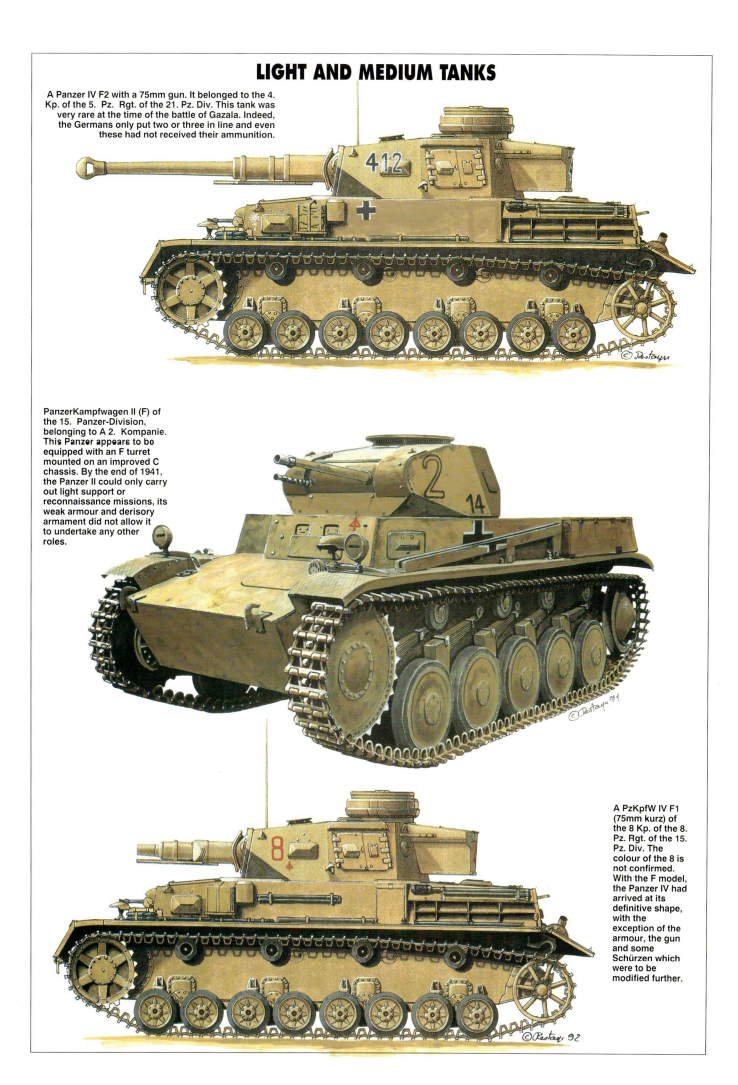

A Panzer IV F2 with a 75mm gun. It belonged to the 4. Kp. of the 5. Pz. Rgt. of the 21. Pz. Div. This tank was very rare at the time of the battle of Gazala. Indeed, the Germans only put two or three in line and even these had not received their ammunition.

PanzerKampfwagen II (F) of the 15. Panzer-Division, belonging to A 2. Kompanie. This Panzer appears to be equipped with an F turret mounted on an improved C chassis. By the end of 1941, the Panzer II could only carry out light support or reconnaissance missions, its weak armour and derisory armament did not allow it to undertake any other roles.

A PzKpfW IV F1 (75mm kurz) of the 8 Kp. of the 8. Pz. Rgt. of the 15. Pz. Div. The colour of the 8 is not confirmed. With the F model, the Panzer IV had arrived at its definitive shape, with the exception of the armour, the gun and some Schürzen which were to be modified further.

GERMAN AND POLISH PANZER III

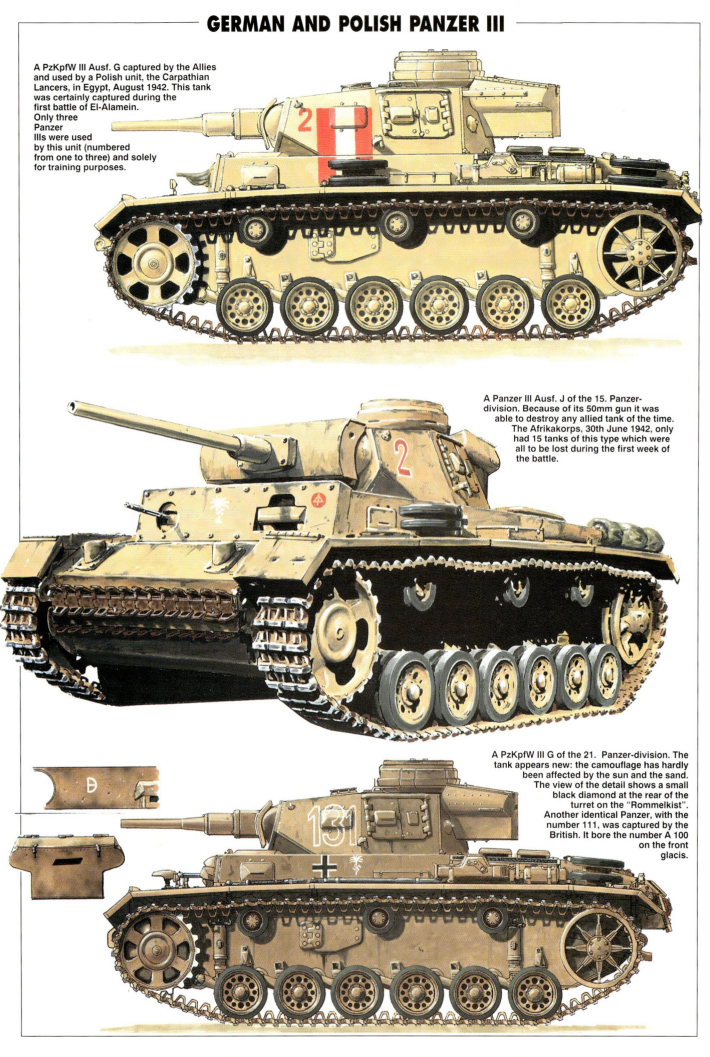

A PzKpfW III Ausf. G captured by the Allies and used by a Polish unit, the Carpathian Lancers, in Egypt, August 1942. This tank was certainly captured during the first battle of El-Alamein. Only three Panzer IIIs were used by this unit (numbered from one to three) and solely for training purposes.

A Panzer III Ausf. J of the 15. Panzer-division. Because of its 50mm gun it was able to destroy any allied tank of the time. The Afrikakorps, 30th June 1942, only had 15 tanks of this type which were all to be lost during the first week of the battle.

A PzKpfW III G of the 21. Panzer-division. The tank appears new: the camouflage has hardly been affected by the sun and the sand. The view of the detail shows a small black diamond at the rear of the turret on the "Rommelkist". Another identical Panzer, with the number 111, was captured by the British. It bore the number A 100 on the front glacis.

DEUTSCHER AFRIKAKORPS PANZER III

A Panzer III G with a 50mm short gun. It belonged to the 3. Kp. of the 5. Pz. Rgt. of the 21. Pz. Div. The tank still bears the large white numbers too visible in the desert. Moreover, the sand yellow seems to have been painted directly on the grey which was the regulation colour on the European front.

A PzKpfW III J (50mm kurz) of the 5. Kp. of the Pz. Rgt. 8 of the 15 Pz. Div. The figure 5 is repeated at the rear of the turret. The DAK palm tree sign is painted to the left of the driver's vision slit.

A Panzer III J of the 1 Kp. of the 8. Pz. Rgt. of the 15. Pz. Div. This tank was one of the first to rejoin the DAK in May 1942. Indeed, at that date, Rommel only had 19 Panzer IIIs with a 50mm long gun at his disposal. The red identification number is repeated at the rear of the turret.

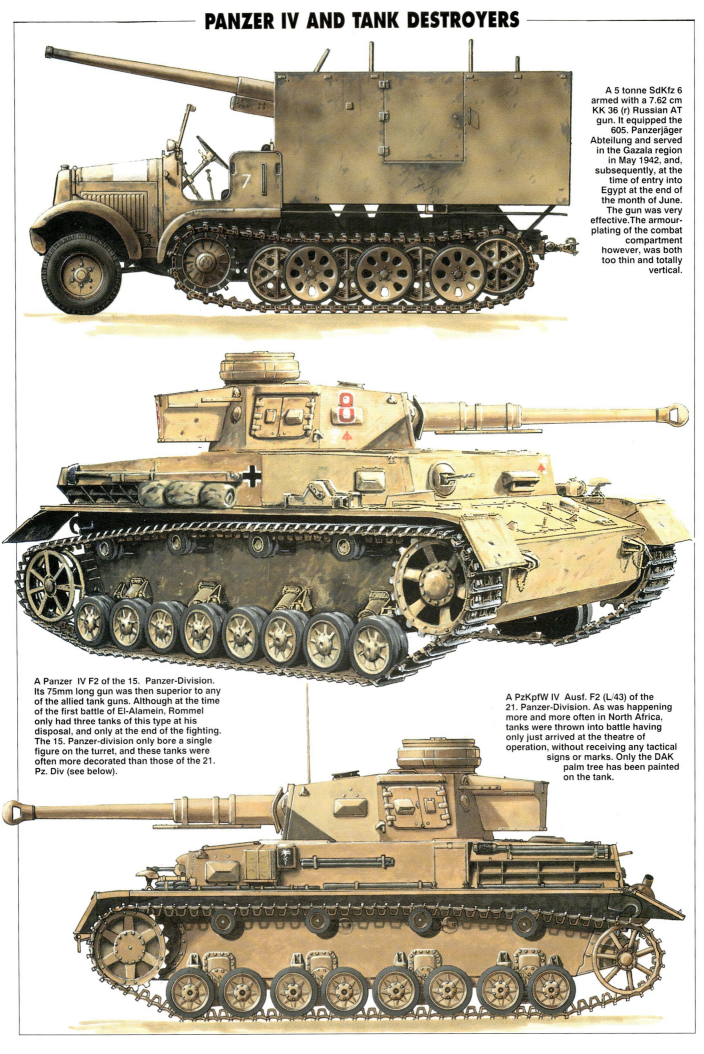

A 5 tonne SdKfz 6 armed with a 7.62 cm KK 36 (r) Russian AT gun. It equipped the 605. Panzerjäger Abteilung and served in the Gazala region in May 1942, and, subsequently, at the time of entry into Egypt at the end of the month of June. The gun was very effective.The armour-plating of the combat compartment however, was both too thin and totally vertical.

A Panzer IV F2 of the 15. Panzer-Division. Its 75mm long gun was then superior to any of the allied tank guns. Although at the time of the first battle of El-Alamein, Rommel only had three tanks of this type at his disposal, and only at the end of the fighting. The 15. Panzer-division only bore a single figure on the turret, and these tanks were often more decorated than those of the 21. Pz. Div (see below).

A PzKpfW IV Ausf. F2 (L/43) of the 21. Panzer-Division. As was happening more and more often in North Africa, tanks were thrown into battle having only just arrived at the theatre of operation, without receiving any tactical signs or marks. Only the DAK palm tree has been painted on the tank.

TRUCKS OF THE PANZERARMEE AFRIKA

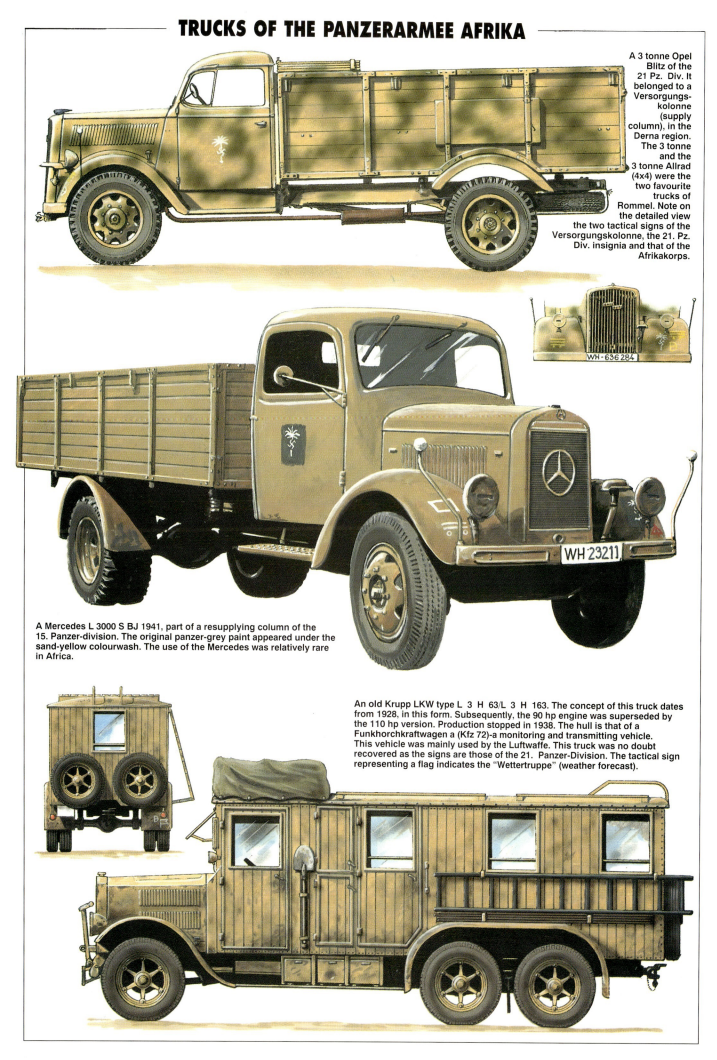

A 3 tonne Opel Blitz of the 21 Pz. Div. It belonged to a Versorgungs-kolonne (supply column), in the Derna region. The 3 tonne and the 3 tonne Allrad (4x4) were the two favourite trucks of Rommel. Note on the detailed view the two tactical signs of the Versorgungskolonne, the 21. Pz. Div. insignia and that of the Afrikakorps.

WH-636 284

A Mercedes L 3000 S BJ 1941, part of a resupplying column of the 15. Panzer-division. The original panzer-grey paint appeared under the sand-yellow colourwash. The use of the Mercedes was relatively rare in Africa.

WH 23211

An old Krupp LKW type L 3 H 63/L 3 H 163. The concept of this truck dates from 1928, in this form. Subsequently, the 90 hp engine was superseded by the 110 hp version. Production stopped in 1938. The hull is that of a Funkhorchkraftwagen a (Kfz 72)-a monitoring and transmitting vehicle. This vehicle was mainly used by the Luftwaffe. This truck was no doubt recovered as the signs are those of the 21. Panzer-Division. The tactical sign representing a flag indicates the "Wettertruppe" (weather forecast).

THE FIRST BRITISH TANKS IN THE DESERT 1940-1941

Light tank Mk II B of the 6th Australian cavalry division, 1940, at the border of Egypt and Libya. The tactical value of this vehicle was minimal and the 10mm armour-plating was almost useless.

British camouflage, complicated to analyse, was constantly evolving. The basic colour was sand-yellow, partially re-covered with stripes of very varied colours; brown and sky-blue were however the most commonly used in the *Western Desert.*

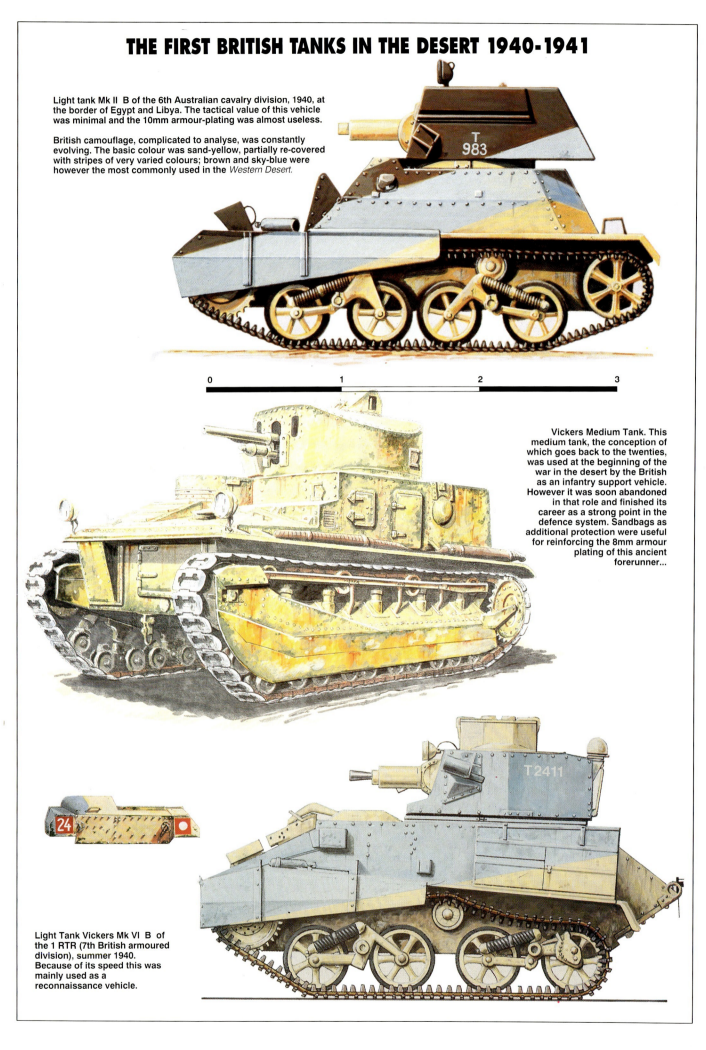

Vickers Medium Tank. This medium tank, the conception of which goes back to the twenties, was used at the beginning of the war in the desert by the British as an infantry support vehicle. However it was soon abandoned in that role and finished its career as a strong point in the defence system. Sandbags as additional protection were useful for reinforcing the 8mm armour plating of this ancient forerunner...

Light Tank Vickers Mk VI B of the 1 RTR (7th British armoured division), summer 1940. Because of its speed this was mainly used as a reconnaissance vehicle.

LIGHT TANKS MARK VI IN EUROPE AND NORTH AFRICA

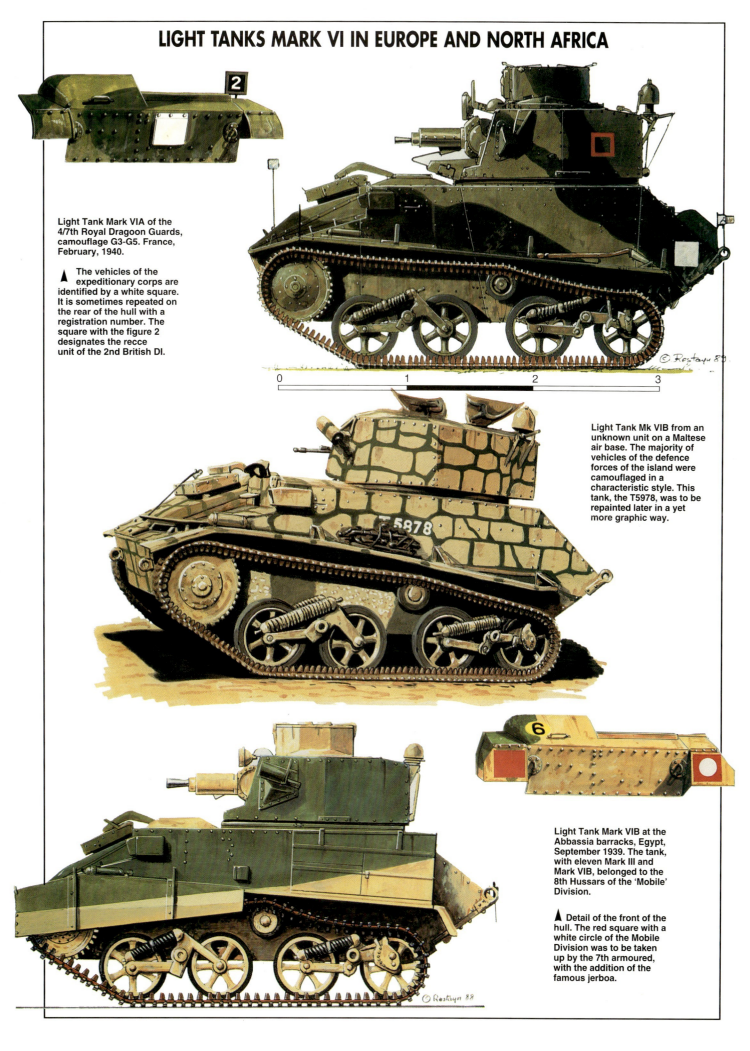

Light Tank Mark VIA of the 4/7th Royal Dragoon Guards, camouflage G3-G5. France, February, 1940.

▲ The vehicles of the expeditionary corps are identified by a white square. It is sometimes repeated on the rear of the hull with a registration number. The square with the figure 2 designates the recce unit of the 2nd British DI.

Light Tank Mk VIB from an unknown unit on a Maltese air base. The majority of vehicles of the defence forces of the island were camouflaged in a characteristic style. This tank, the T5978, was to be repainted later in a yet more graphic way.

Light Tank Mark VIB at the Abbassia barracks, Egypt, September 1939. The tank, with eleven Mark III and Mark VIB, belonged to the 8th Hussars of the 'Mobile' Division.

▲ Detail of the front of the hull. The red square with a white circle of the Mobile Division was to be taken up by the 7th armoured, with the addition of the famous jerboa.

FRENCH AND BRITISH AFVs IN AFRICA, 1940-1941

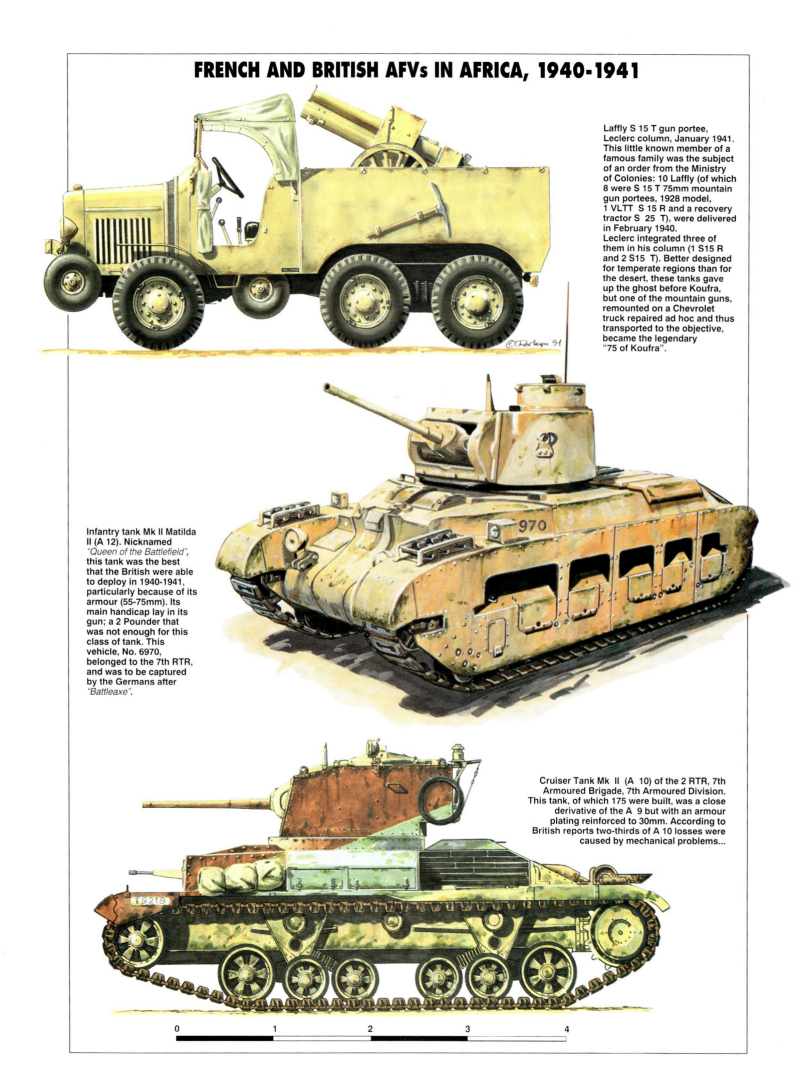

Laffly S 15 T gun portee, Leclerc column, January 1941. This little known member of a famous family was the subject of an order from the Ministry of Colonies: 10 Laffly (of which 8 were S 15 T 75mm mountain gun portees, 1928 model, 1 VLTT S 15 R and a recovery tractor S 25 T), were delivered in February 1940.
Leclerc integrated three of them in his column (1 S15 R and 2 S15 T). Better designed for temperate regions than for the desert, these tanks gave up the ghost before Koufra, but one of the mountain guns, remounted on a Chevrolet truck repaired ad hoc and thus transported to the objective, became the legendary "75 of Koufra".

Infantry tank Mk II Matilda II (A 12). Nicknamed *"Queen of the Battlefield"*, this tank was the best that the British were able to deploy in 1940-1941, particularly because of its armour (55-75mm). Its main handicap lay in its gun; a 2 Pounder that was not enough for this class of tank. This vehicle, No. 6970, belonged to the 7th RTR, and was to be captured by the Germans after *"Battleaxe"*.

Cruiser Tank Mk II (A 10) of the 2 RTR, 7th Armoured Brigade, 7th Armoured Division. This tank, of which 175 were built, was a close derivative of the A 9 but with an armour plating reinforced to 30mm. According to British reports two-thirds of A 10 losses were caused by mechanical problems...

0   1   2   3   4

BRITISH INFANTRY TANKS

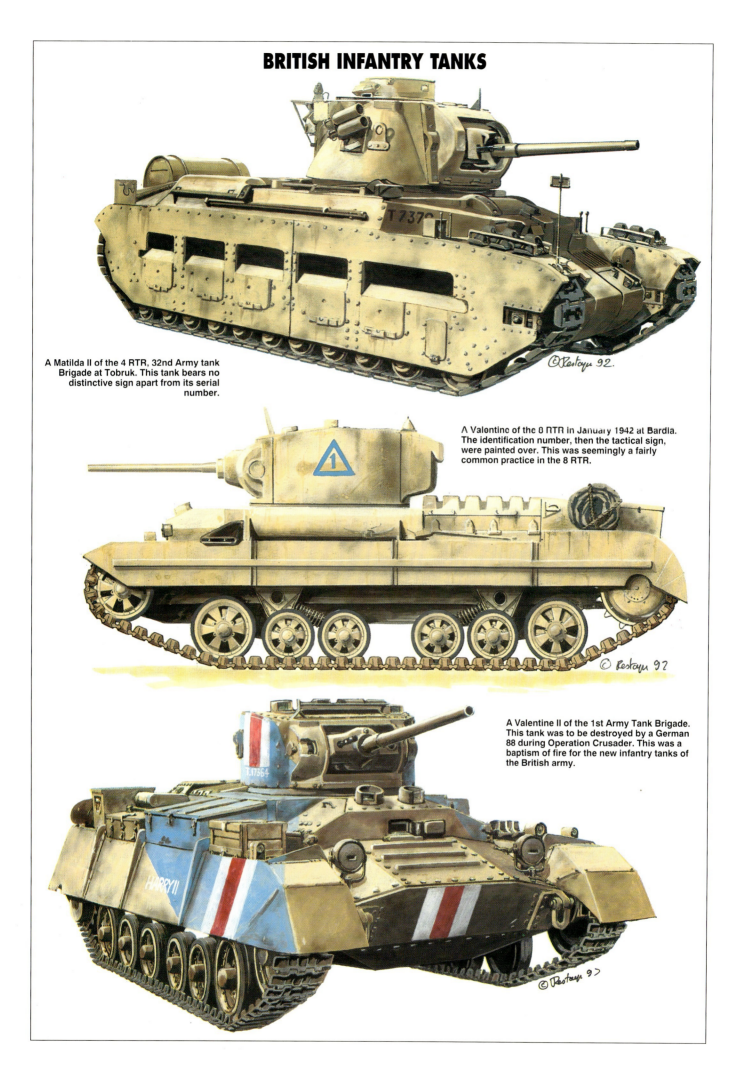

A Matilda II of the 4 RTR, 32nd Army tank Brigade at Tobruk. This tank bears no distinctive sign apart from its serial number.

A Valentine of the 8 RTR in January 1942 at Bardia. The identification number, then the tactical sign, were painted over. This was seemingly a fairly common practice in the 8 RTR.

A Valentine II of the 1st Army Tank Brigade. This tank was to be destroyed by a German 88 during Operation Crusader. This was a baptism of fire for the new infantry tanks of the British army.

BRITISH 8TH ARMY AFVs

Matilda Mk II of the 7 RTR. Captured intact by the Germans, it was immediately taken back again, as the shortage of tanks was the scourge of the Afrikakorps. The name *Gazelle III* leads us to the conclusion that *Gazelle I* and *II* did not meet with a more enviable fate.

A Dorchester AEC Armoured Command vehicle of the HQ of the 2nd Armoured Division. Because of its comfortable dimensions, the captured Dorchesters were highly valued by the German Generals. Rommel, Streich and Crüwell used it, under the name of *"Mammoth"*, as command vehicles. The camouflage is desert *yellow*, light blue and green/black. The figure 3 is repeated on each side of the vehicle at the rear.

An A 13 Cruiser of the 2 Royal Tank Regiment, end of November 1941. The old light blue camouflage reappeared under the layer of *desert yellow* paint.

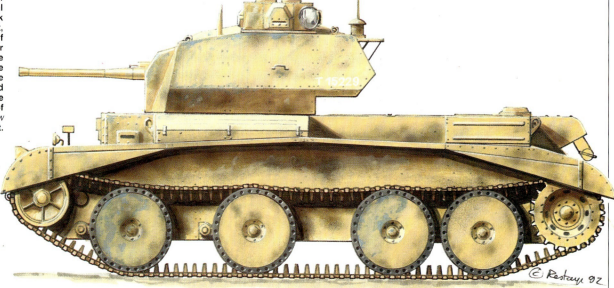

INFANTRY TANK MATILDA II

"Gorgonzola" was a 7 RTR Matilda II in May 1940 on the French front. It was camouflaged in two shades of green. The name of the tank is repeated on the hull at the rear. The white square was the nationality mark of all BEF vehicles in 1939-1940.

A Matilda II of the 7 RTR during the capture of Bardia in January 1941. The tank was re-covered with *"Caunter Camouflage"* sand, green and black typical of the first year of the war in the desert. The white-red-white reconnaissance stripes are especially visible on the hull and the turret.

A Matilda II of the 32nd Army Tank Brigade in March 1942. This tank of the 4 Royal Tank Regiment served in the defence of Tobruk, a role to which the Matilda was just about adapted at that time. In fact, its slowness meant it did not participate in operations over long distances in the desert. The green colour used in Europe is still visible under the sand coloured coat.

CRUSADER AND LIGHT VEHICLES OF THE 8TH ARMY

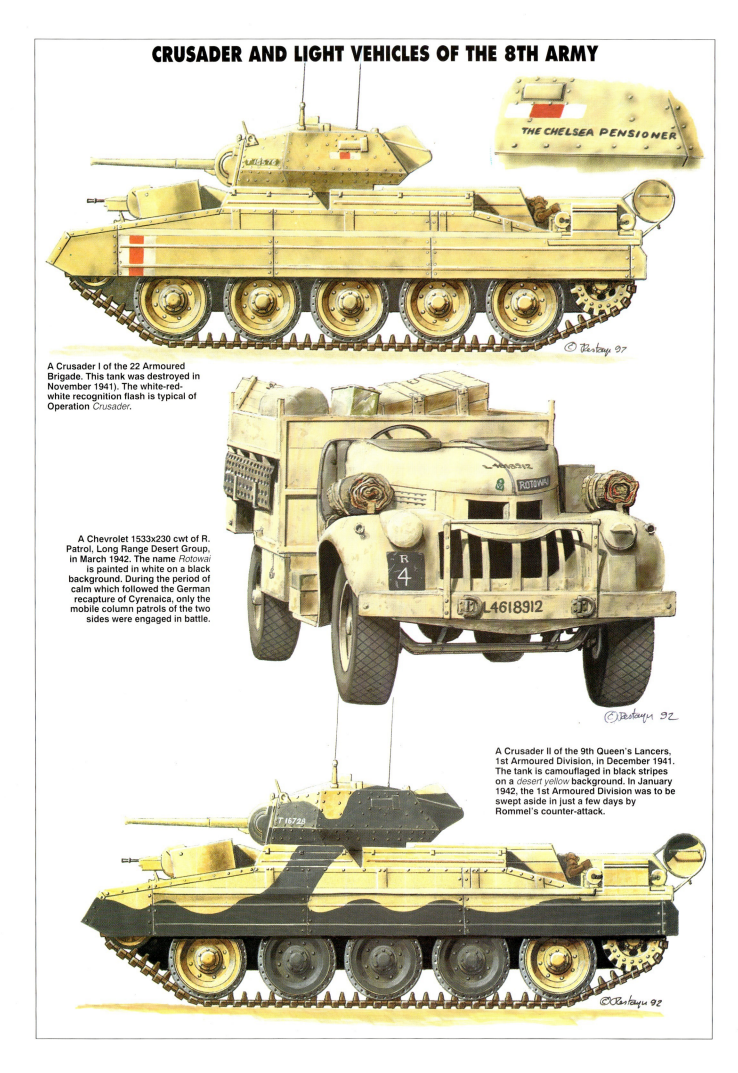

THE CHELSEA PENSIONER

A Crusader I of the 22 Armoured Brigade. This tank was destroyed in November 1941). The white-red-white recognition flash is typical of Operation *Crusader*.

A Chevrolet 1533x230 cwt of R. Patrol, Long Range Desert Group, in March 1942. The name *Rotowai* is painted in white on a black background. During the period of calm which followed the German recapture of Cyrenaica, only the mobile column patrols of the two sides were engaged in battle.

A Crusader II of the 9th Queen's Lancers, 1st Armoured Division, in December 1941. The tank is camouflaged in black stripes on a *desert yellow* background. In January 1942, the 1st Armoured Division was to be swept aside in just a few days by Rommel's counter-attack.

8TH ARMY CRUSADERS

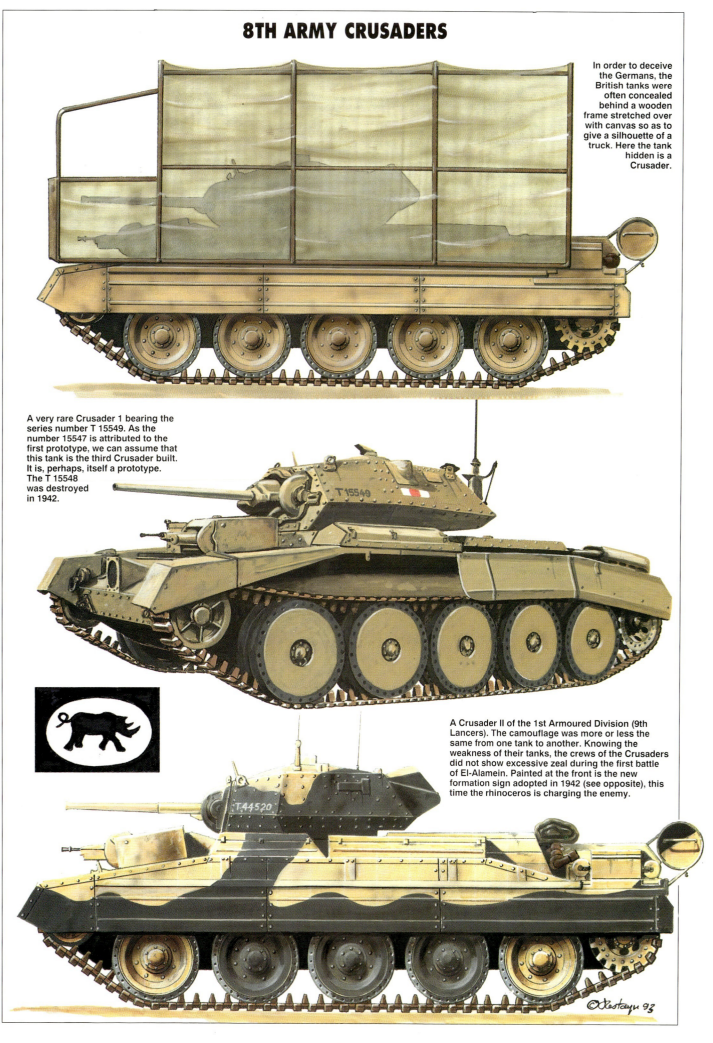

In order to deceive the Germans, the British tanks were often concealed behind a wooden frame stretched over with canvas so as to give a silhouette of a truck. Here the tank hidden is a Crusader.

A very rare Crusader 1 bearing the series number T 15549. As the number 15547 is attributed to the first prototype, we can assume that this tank is the third Crusader built. It is, perhaps, itself a prototype. The T 15548 was destroyed in 1942.

A Crusader II of the 1st Armoured Division (9th Lancers). The camouflage was more or less the same from one tank to another. Knowing the weakness of their tanks, the crews of the Crusaders did not show excessive zeal during the first battle of El-Alamein. Painted at the front is the new formation sign adopted in 1942 (see opposite), this time the rhinoceros is charging the enemy.

AMERICAN TANKS DELIVERED TO THE 8TH ARMY

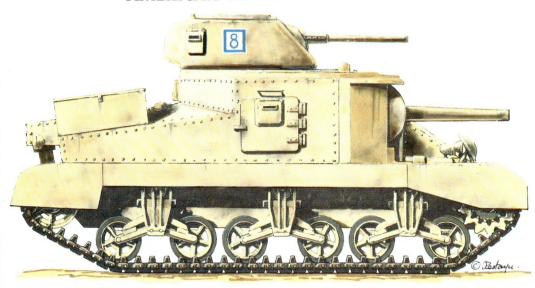

A Grant of the 1st
Armoured Division.
It belonged to a
D squadron of a
non-identified unit.
This tank was to be
destroyed at the battle
of Gazala.

A Grant of the 2nd Royal
Gloucestershire Hussars,
22nd Armoured Brigade,
during the battle of Gazala.
No insignia are apparent on
this tank.

An M3 Stuart of the 3
RTR, Libya, March-
April 1942. This tank
belonged to the A
squadron of the
battalion. It is painted
in *desert yellow*. On
the eve of the battle
of Gazala the Stuarts
were rejoined by
some Grants in some
mixed units, this
allowed them to
compensate for their
weak arms.

T.37752

BRITISH TANKS

A Grant of the 7th Armoured Division. The figure "86" indicates a tank of the 1st armoured brigade, 2nd regiment. In July 1942, the 7th Armoured Division no longer had a single medium tank and this one had very likely just been assigned to the 1st Armoured Division.

Devoid of any divisional insignia, this Grant was commissioned with the 1st Armoured Division. The turret marking indicates that it was on the strength of 3 Troop, A Squadron.

A Valentine of the 4 RTR destroyed during the second battle of Ruweisat. It belonged to the 32nd Army Tank Brigade, which was entirely destroyed 22nd July. The eye on the turret reminds us of the Royal Tank Regiment legend, during the first world war, a Chinese labourer asked: *"How can the tanks see without eyes?"*.

THE M3 LEE/GRANT MEDIUM TANK , 1942

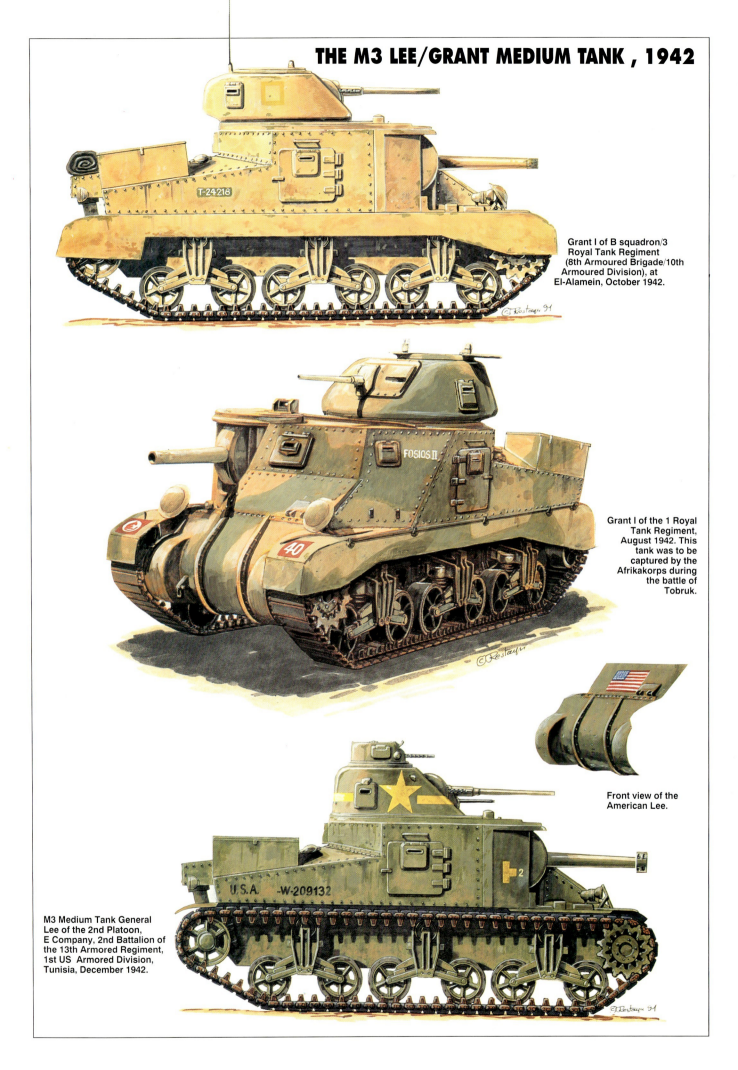

Grant I of B squadron/3
Royal Tank Regiment
(8th Armoured Brigade/10th
Armoured Division), at
El-Alamein, October 1942.

Grant I of the 1 Royal
Tank Regiment,
August 1942. This
tank was to be
captured by the
Afrikakorps during
the battle of
Tobruk.

Front view of the
American Lee.

M3 Medium Tank General
Lee of the 2nd Platoon,
E Company, 2nd Battalion of
the 13th Armored Regiment,
1st US Armored Division,
Tunisia, December 1942.

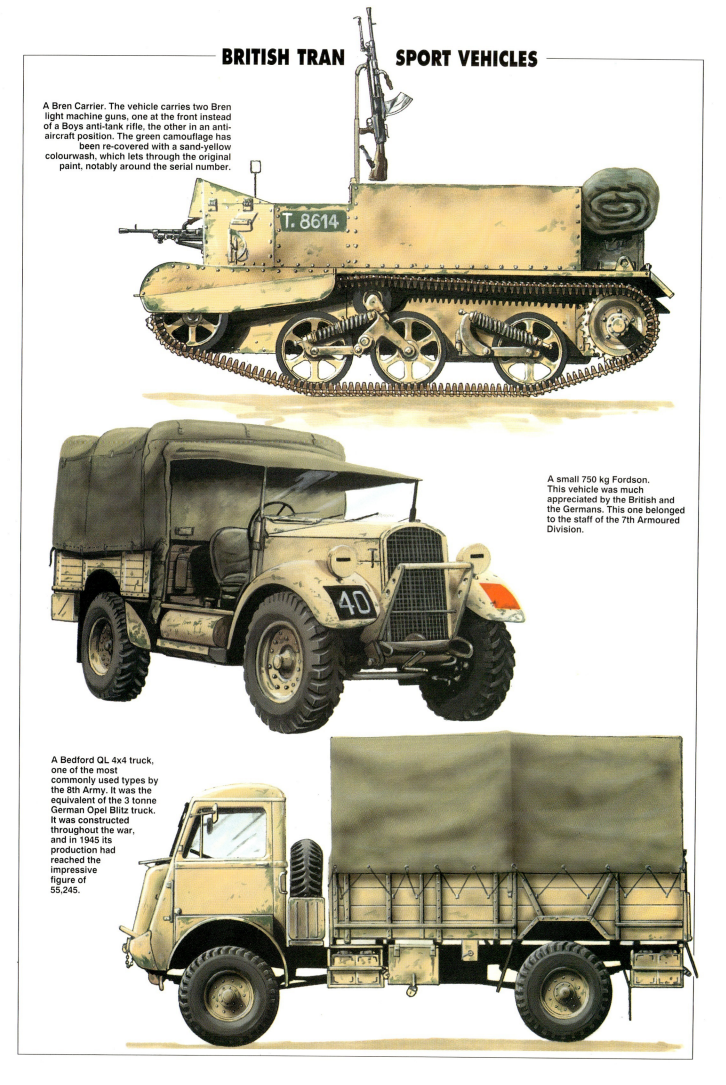

A Bren Carrier. The vehicle carries two Bren light machine guns, one at the front instead of a Boys anti-tank rifle, the other in an anti-aircraft position. The green camouflage has been re-covered with a sand-yellow colourwash, which lets through the original paint, notably around the serial number.

T. 8614

A small 750 kg Fordson. This vehicle was much appreciated by the British and the Germans. This one belonged to the staff of the 7th Armoured Division.

A Bedford QL 4x4 truck, one of the most commonly used types by the 8th Army. It was the equivalent of the 3 tonne German Opel Blitz truck. It was constructed throughout the war, and in 1945 its production had reached the impressive figure of 55,245.

1941

THE

EASTERN

FRONT

LIGHT GERMAN AFVs

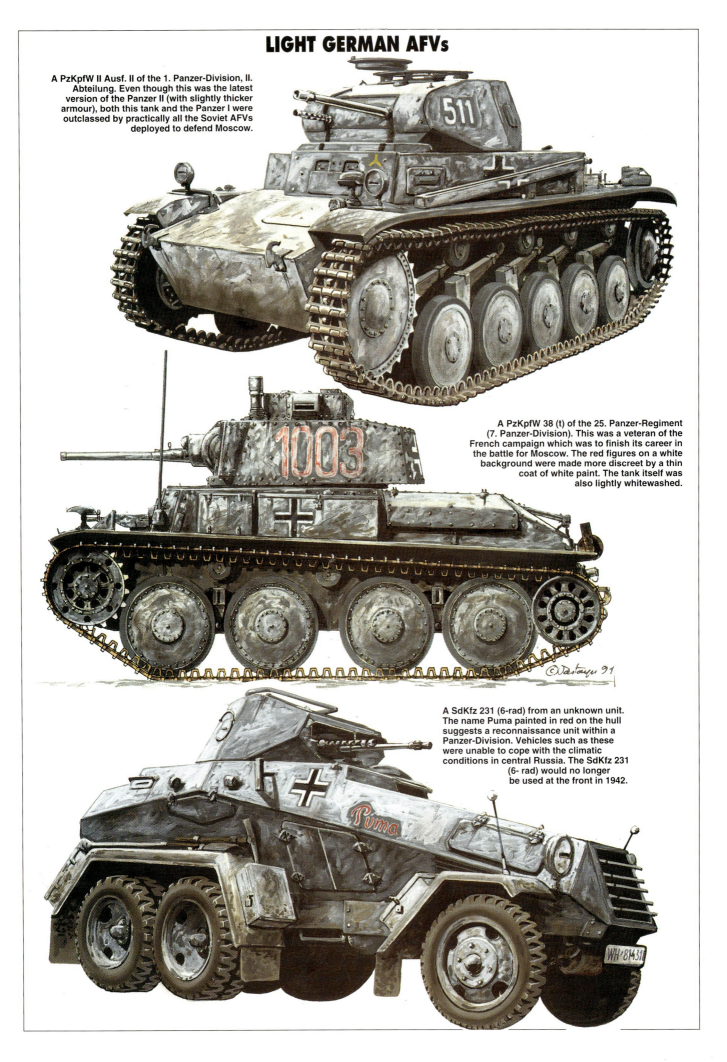

A PzKpfW II Ausf. II of the 1. Panzer-Division, II. Abteilung. Even though this was the latest version of the Panzer II (with slightly thicker armour), both this tank and the Panzer I were outclassed by practically all the Soviet AFVs deployed to defend Moscow.

A PzKpfW 38 (t) of the 25. Panzer-Regiment (7. Panzer-Division). This was a veteran of the French campaign which was to finish its career in the battle for Moscow. The red figures on a white background were made more discreet by a thin coat of white paint. The tank itself was also lightly whitewashed.

A SdKfz 231 (6-rad) from an unknown unit. The name Puma painted in red on the hull suggests a reconnaissance unit within a Panzer-Division. Vehicles such as these were unable to cope with the climatic conditions in central Russia. The SdKfz 231 (6- rad) would no longer be used at the front in 1942.

GERMAN ARMOURED VEHICLES, SPRING 1941

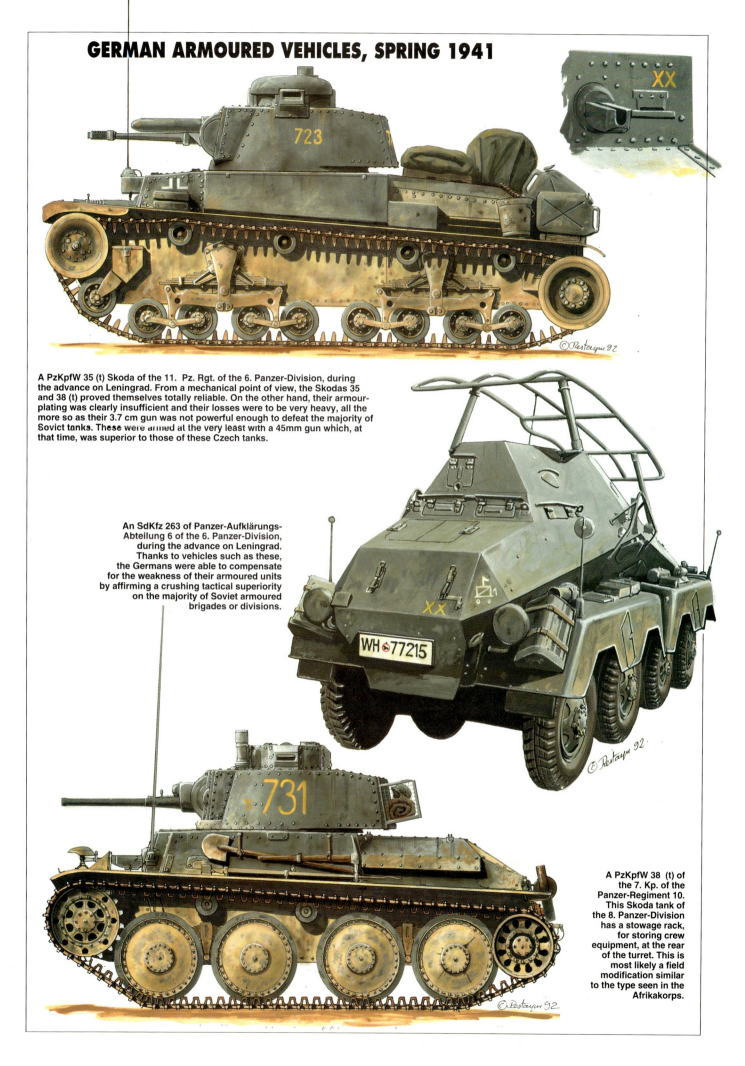

A PzKpfW 35 (t) Skoda of the 11. Pz. Rgt. of the 6. Panzer-Division, during the advance on Leningrad. From a mechanical point of view, the Skodas 35 and 38 (t) proved themselves totally reliable. On the other hand, their armour-plating was clearly insufficient and their losses were to be very heavy, all the more so as their 3.7 cm gun was not powerful enough to defeat the majority of Soviet tanks. These were armed at the very least with a 45mm gun which, at that time, was superior to those of these Czech tanks.

An SdKfz 263 of Panzer-Aufklärungs-Abteilung 6 of the 6. Panzer-Division, during the advance on Leningrad. Thanks to vehicles such as these, the Germans were able to compensate for the weakness of their armoured units by affirming a crushing tactical superiority on the majority of Soviet armoured brigades or divisions.

A PzKpfW 38 (t) of the 7. Kp. of the Panzer-Regiment 10. This Skoda tank of the 8. Panzer-Division has a stowage rack, for storing crew equipment, at the rear of the turret. This is most likely a field modification similar to the type seen in the Afrikakorps.

LIGHT GERMAN TANKS, SPRING 1941

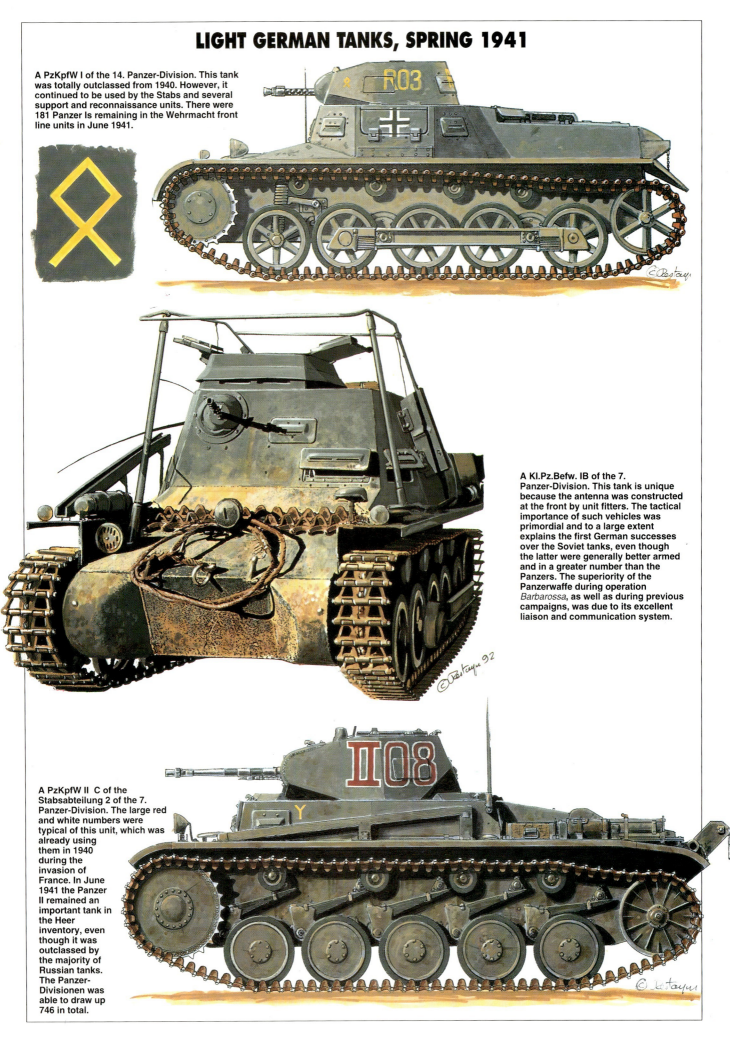

A PzKpfW I of the 14. Panzer-Division. This tank was totally outclassed from 1940. However, it continued to be used by the Stabs and several support and reconnaissance units. There were 181 Panzer Is remaining in the Wehrmacht front line units in June 1941.

A Kl.Pz.Befw. IB of the 7. Panzer-Division. This tank is unique because the antenna was constructed at the front by unit fitters. The tactical importance of such vehicles was primordial and to a large extent explains the first German successes over the Soviet tanks, even though the latter were generally better armed and in a greater number than the Panzers. The superiority of the Panzerwaffe during operation *Barbarossa*, as well as during previous campaigns, was due to its excellent liaison and communication system.

A PzKpfW II C of the Stabsabteilung 2 of the 7. Panzer-Division. The large red and white numbers were typical of this unit, which was already using them in 1940 during the invasion of France. In June 1941 the Panzer II remained an important tank in the Heer inventory, even though it was outclassed by the majority of Russian tanks. The Panzer-Divisionen was able to draw up 746 in total.

GERMAN MEDIUM TANKS, SPRINGS 1941

A PzKpfW III Ausf. H of Panzer Regiment 33 (9. Panzer-Division). This tank was used during fighting in the Biala Zerklev region, south of Kiev, mid-July 1941. The 5cm KwK/L42 gun had not at that time been mounted on all the Panzer III. Even though it was superior to the 3.7cm used in the first campaigns, the 5cm gun was clearly inferior to the T-34's. The KwK/L42 was capable of destroying a T-34 from about 800m. On the other hand the T-34 7.62mm could destroy a Pz III from about 1500m.

A Panzer IV Ausführung D of the 1. Panzer-Division, during operations against the Luga bridgehead, 13th July 1941. Likc all vehicles of the division, the figures are in white (here 423) and repeated at the rear of the turret.
The divisional sign was changed after the French campaign, the oak leaf being replaced by the three-pointed star, painted in yellow.

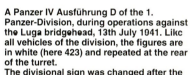

A PzKpfW III Ausf. E/F of the II. Abteilung of the 13. Panzer-Division. The 3.7cm gun was no match for the majority of Russian tanks, even the T-26 had a 45mm gun. Even though the Germans started replacing the 3.7cm with the 5cm prior to operation Barbarossa, there were still many Panzer III with their original armament fighting in the campaign.

PANZER III

The Panzer-Befehlswagen III of Oberst Koll, commanding officer of Panzer-Regiment 11 (6. Panzer-Division) from October 1941. The grey paint was recovered with whitewash which flaked off in the most exposed areas on the tank. The white RO6 mark is repeated on the rear of the turret.

A PzKpfW III Ausf. G of the 1. Panzer-Division, II. Abteilung. Its 50mm short gun was too weak against the KV 1. To destroy a T-34, it needed to get as close as possible to its target, thus taking the risk of being destroyed first.

A PzKpfW III Ausf. E/F of the I. Abteilung of the 5. Pz. Div. The red figures and the unit insignia were left visible. On the other hand, the devil's head was recovered as it was apparently too visible on a white background.

STURMGESCHÜTZ AND PANZER IVs

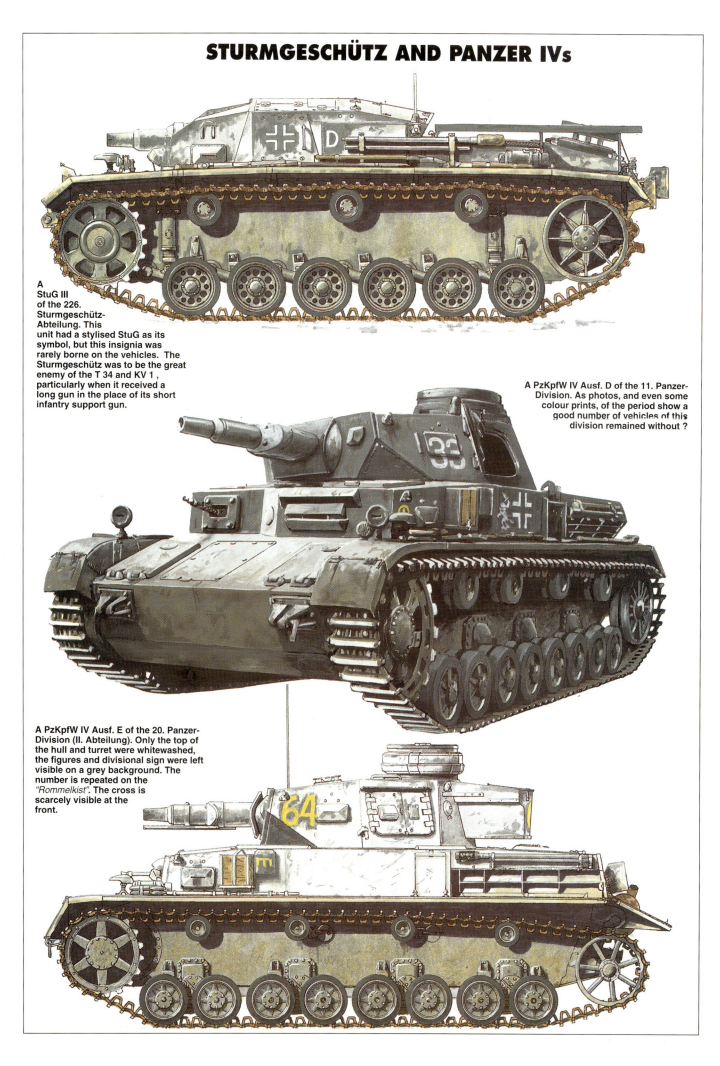

A StuG III of the 226. Sturmgeschütz-Abteilung. This unit had a stylised StuG as its symbol, but this insignia was rarely borne on the vehicles. The Sturmgeschütz was to be the great enemy of the T 34 and KV 1, particularly when it received a long gun in the place of its short infantry support gun.

A PzKpfW IV Ausf. D of the 11. Panzer-Division. As photos, and even some colour prints, of the period show a good number of vehicles of this division remained without ?

A PzKpfW IV Ausf. E of the 20. Panzer-Division (II. Abteilung). Only the top of the hull and turret were whitewashed, the figures and divisional sign were left visible on a grey background. The number is repeated on the *"Rommelkist"*. The cross is scarcely visible at the front.

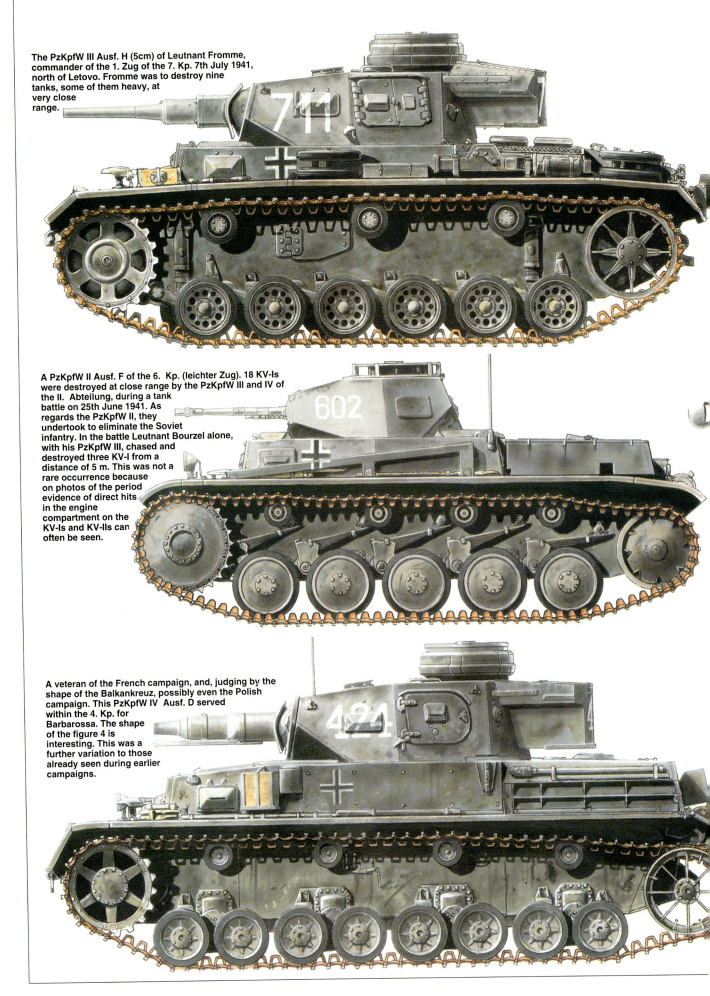

The PzKpfW III Ausf. H (5cm) of Leutnant Fromme, commander of the 1. Zug of the 7. Kp. 7th July 1941, north of Letovo. Fromme was to destroy nine tanks, some of them heavy, at very close range.

A PzKpfW II Ausf. F of the 6. Kp. (leichter Zug). 18 KV-Is were destroyed at close range by the PzKpfW III and IV of the II. Abteilung, during a tank battle on 25th June 1941. As regards the PzKpfW II, they undertook to eliminate the Soviet infantry. In the battle Leutnant Bourzel alone, with his PzKpfW III, chased and destroyed three KV-I from a distance of 5 m. This was not a rare occurrence because on photos of the period evidence of direct hits in the engine compartment on the KV-Is and KV-IIs can often be seen.

A veteran of the French campaign, and, judging by the shape of the Balkankreuz, possibly even the Polish campaign. This PzKpfW IV Ausf. D served within the 4. Kp. for Barbarossa. The shape of the figure 4 is interesting. This was a further variation to those already seen during earlier campaigns.

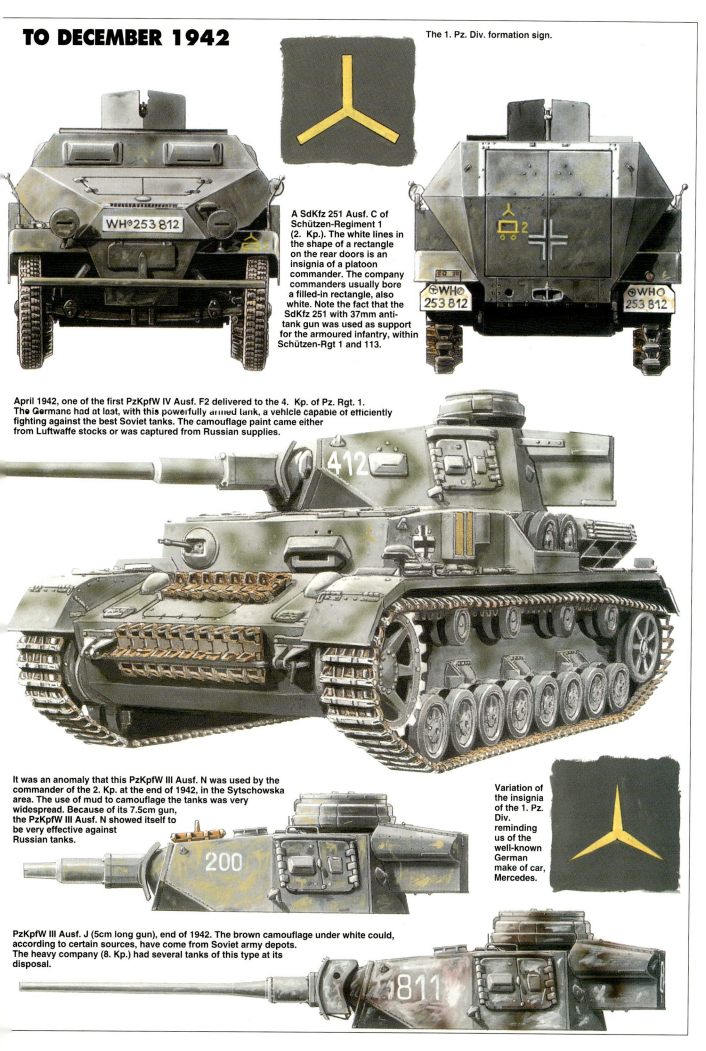

TO DECEMBER 1942

The 1. Pz. Div. formation sign.

A SdKfz 251 Ausf. C of Schützen-Regiment 1 (2. Kp.). The white lines in the shape of a rectangle on the rear doors is an insignia of a platoon commander. The company commanders usually bore a filled-in rectangle, also white. Note the fact that the SdKfz 251 with 37mm anti-tank gun was used as support for the armoured infantry, within Schützen-Rgt 1 and 113.

April 1942, one of the first PzKpfW IV Ausf. F2 delivered to the 4. Kp. of Pz. Rgt. 1. The Germans had at last, with this powerfully armed tank, a vehicle capable of efficiently fighting against the best Soviet tanks. The camouflage paint came either from Luftwaffe stocks or was captured from Russian supplies.

It was an anomaly that this PzKpfW III Ausf. N was used by the commander of the 2. Kp. at the end of 1942, in the Sytschowska area. The use of mud to camouflage the tanks was very widespread. Because of its 7.5cm gun, the PzKpfW III Ausf. N showed itself to be very effective against Russian tanks.

Variation of the insignia of the 1. Pz. Div. reminding us of the well-known German make of car, Mercedes.

PzKpfW III Ausf. J (5cm long gun), end of 1942. The brown camouflage under white could, according to certain sources, have come from Soviet army depots. The heavy company (8. Kp.) had several tanks of this type at its disposal.

DIVERSE GERMAN ARMOURED VEHICLES, SPRING 1941

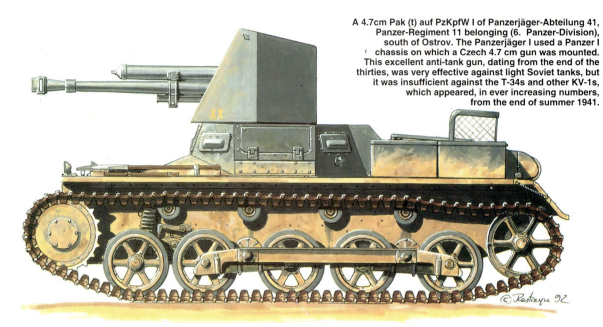

A 4.7cm Pak (t) auf PzKpfW I of Panzerjäger-Abteilung 41, Panzer-Regiment 11 belonging (6. Panzer-Division), south of Ostrov. The Panzerjäger I used a Panzer I chassis on which a Czech 4.7 cm gun was mounted. This excellent anti-tank gun, dating from the end of the thirties, was very effective against light Soviet tanks, but it was insufficient against the T-34s and other KV-1s, which appeared, in ever increasing numbers, from the end of summer 1941.

An SdKfz 250 of the Panzer-Pionier- Btl. 37 of the 1. Panzer-Division. This AFV was used outside Leningrad in September 1941. Its white tactical symbol indicates that it was a command vehicle from a Nebelwerfer battery.

A StuG II C of Sturmgeschütz-Abteilung 201 in the Terespol region, near Moscow, October 1941. This vehicle, which used a three-figure registration system as in the tank units, was one of the 272 Sturmgeschütze which took part in operation Barbarossa. Little by little, the StuG III was to reveal itself to be a formidable AFV, which, furthermore, was less costly to build than a tank. In 1944, it was often used within the Panzer-Division, whereas in 1941 it was only used in autonomous units.

THE PANZERJÄGER MARDER III

A Panzerjäger Marder III (SdKfz 139, 7.62mm Russian gun) of the 1. Panzer-Division (37. Panzerjäger-Abteilung). Notice the figure 1 near the tactical sign, designating the company; and the figure 3, the vehicle number, painted near the cross. The Marder III reached the Panzergrenadier and anti-tank units from 1942, in North Africa and, as here, on the Eastern front.

A Panzerjäger Marder III of the 15. Panzer-Division (33. Panzerjäger-Abteilung), first vehicle of the Stab of the 3rd company. Sixty-six of this first variation of the Marder III arrived in North Africa between July and November 1942. The Soviet gun, used while waiting for the availability of the Pak 40, remained an excellent arm which compensated for an insufficient mobility and limited crew protection. The high outline is very noticeable on this picture.

Panzerjäger Marder III (ausf. H, Pak 40 AT gun) of the 9. Panzer-Division (50. Panzerjäger-Abteilung). The tank was re-covered with sand-coloured paint and green patches. The formation sign positioned on the mantlet is yellow, the figures and the cross are white. Operation Zitadelle, Kursk salient, USSR, July 1943. The Marder remained an SP anti-tank gun until the arrival of the Jagdpanzer 38 (Hetzer) based on the same chassis.

THE PANZERJÄGER MARDER III AUSF. M

Kfz Sd Kfz 138
Leergew: 20 200 Kg
Ver Kl. 5

The Marder III depicted here is how it would look just after leaving the factory. Its camouflage is typical; two different shades of sand-colour. It was to be painted in a more effective way at the theatre of operations by the Panzerjäger-Abteilung mechanics. This particular tank was seen on manoeuvres, Bremen region, winter 1943-1944. The fighting compartment's top sides have apparently been protected by a tarpaulin, hence the difference in colour.

A Marder III of Panzerjäger-Abteilung 37 (1. Panzer-Division) west of Budapest, Hungary, during the winter of 1944-1945. The tank is whitewashed but both the tactical mark (repeated on the rear of the hull, to the right, see detail above) and the national emblem remain visible.

A Marder III of Panzerjäger-Abteilung 561, summer 1944 on the Eastern front. It bears no nationality emblem, only the name *Gerda* or *Gerdi* is visible on the left flank. Another Marder of the unit (No. 241) bears the name *Löwe* or *Lolli* on the right side. The camouflage is typical of this period.

GERDA

211

THE SDKFZ 232, 233 AND 263 ARMOURED CARS, 1939-1943

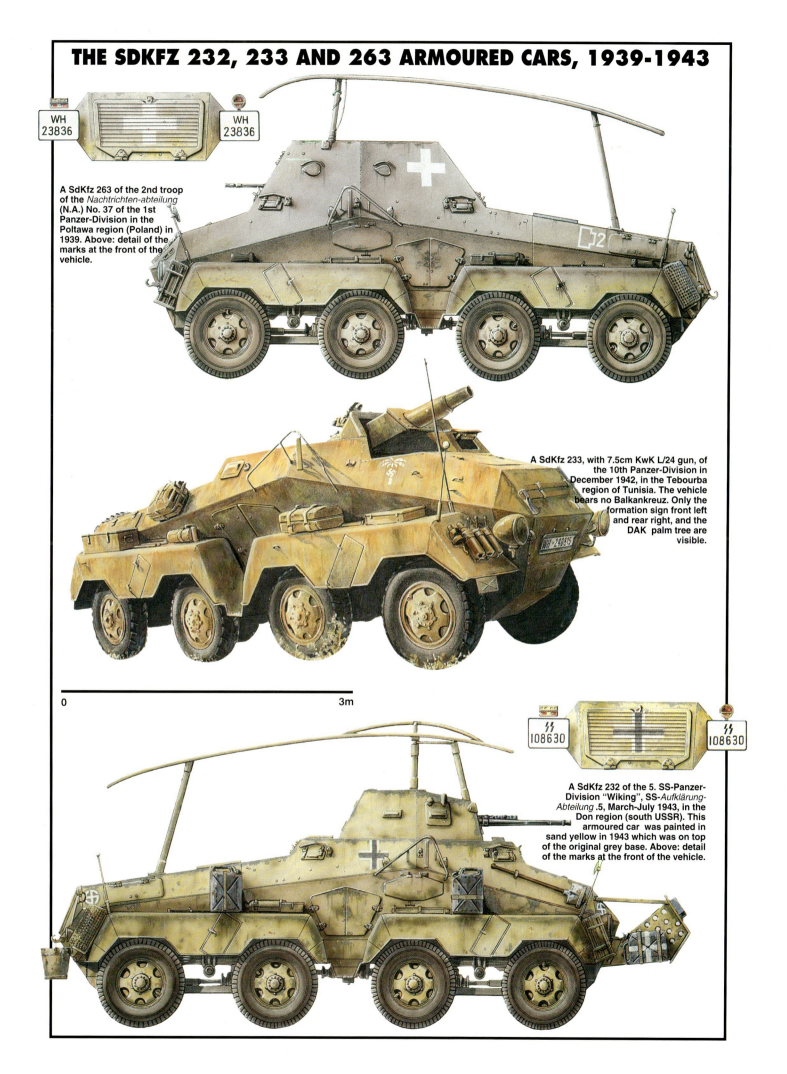

WH 23836 | WH 23836

A SdKfz 263 of the 2nd troop of the *Nachtrichten-abteilung* (N.A.) No. 37 of the 1st Panzer-Division in the Poltawa region (Poland) in 1939. Above: detail of the marks at the front of the vehicle.

A SdKfz 233, with 7.5cm KwK L/24 gun, of the 10th Panzer-Division in December 1942, in the Tebourba region of Tunisia. The vehicle bears no Balkankreuz. Only the formation sign front left and rear right, and the DAK palm tree are visible.

0   3m

ϟϟ 108630 | ϟϟ 108630

A SdKfz 232 of the 5. SS-Panzer-Division "Wiking", SS-*Aufklärung-Abteilung* .5, March-July 1943, in the Don region (south USSR). This armoured car was painted in sand yellow in 1943 which was on top of the original grey base. Above: detail of the marks at the front of the vehicle.

A SdKfz 251 B of the 1. Pz. Div. (Schützen-Regiment 113), Panzerkorps Guderian, during the French campaign *(see details of the vehicle below)*.

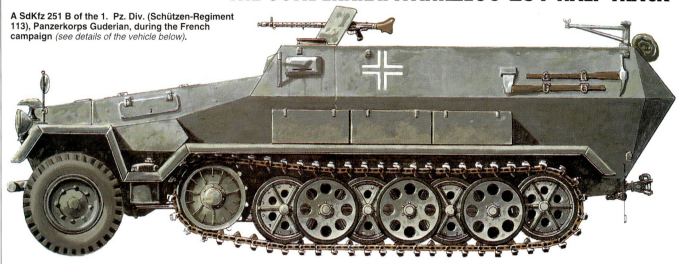

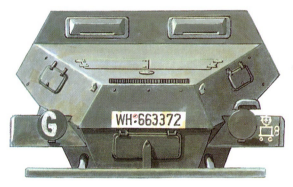

Front and rear views of the vehicle described above.

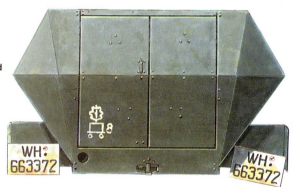

Opposite. The new insignia was a crossed circle, here in yellow on the right mud-guard. White stripes are painted at the two ends of the mud-guards.

SdKfz 251 B of the 11. Pz. Div. (Schützen-Regiment 110) during operations in the Balkans. Notice the two different formation signs of the division, borne concurrently on the mud-guards. This traditional and distinctive insignia is reproduced in detail

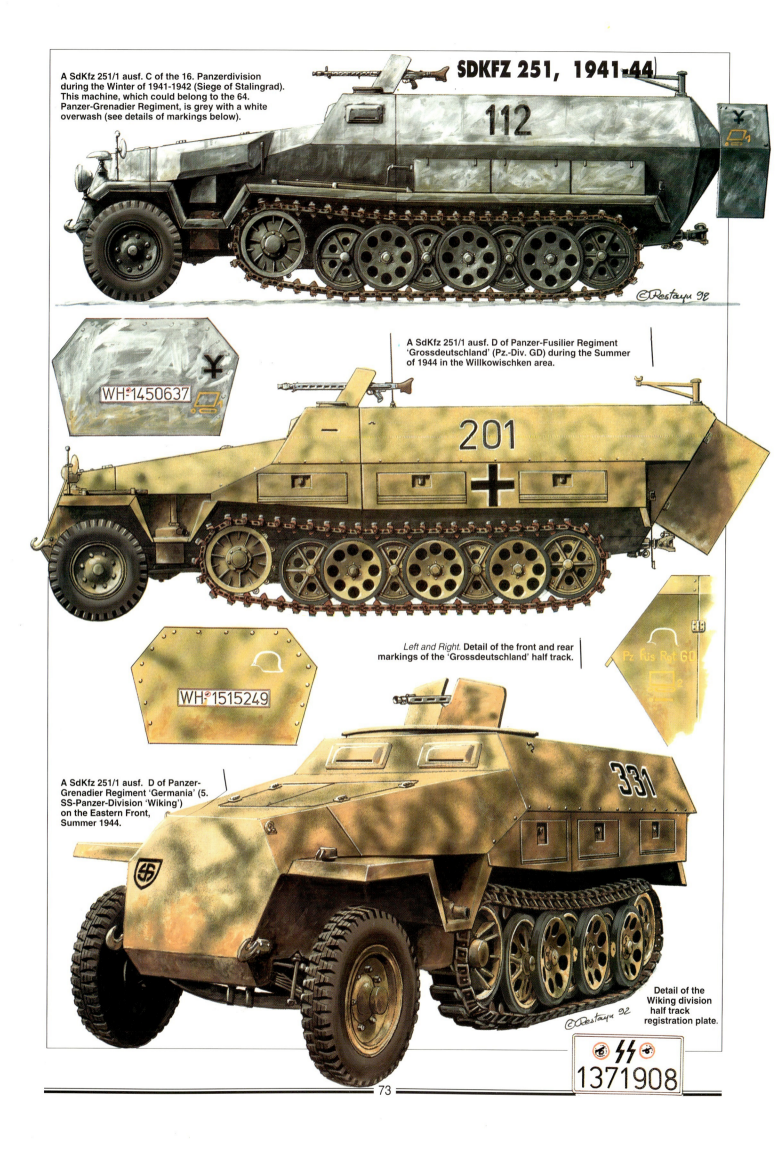

SDKFZ 251, 1941-44

A SdKfz 251/1 ausf. C of the 16. Panzerdivision during the Winter of 1941-1942 (Siege of Stalingrad). This machine, which could belong to the 64. Panzer-Grenadier Regiment, is grey with a white overwash (see details of markings below).

WH·1450637

A SdKfz 251/1 ausf. D of Panzer-Fusilier Regiment 'Grossdeutschland' (Pz.-Div. GD) during the Summer of 1944 in the Willkowischken area.

201

Left and Right. **Detail of the front and rear markings of the 'Grossdeutschland' half track.**

Pz Füs Rgt GD

WH·1515249

A SdKfz 251/1 ausf. D of Panzer-Grenadier Regiment 'Germania' (5. SS-Panzer-Division 'Wiking') on the Eastern Front, Summer 1944.

331

Detail of the Wiking division half track registration plate.

SS 1371908

RUSSIAN TANKS CAPTURED BY THE GERMANS

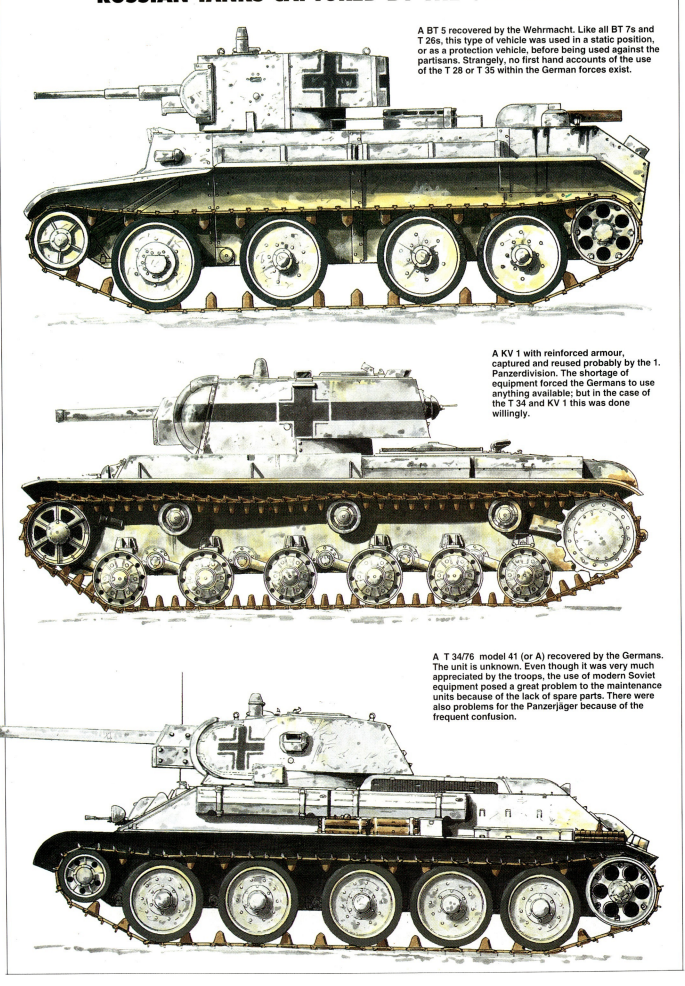

A BT 5 recovered by the Wehrmacht. Like all BT 7s and T 26s, this type of vehicle was used in a static position, or as a protection vehicle, before being used against the partisans. Strangely, no first hand accounts of the use of the T 28 or T 35 within the German forces exist.

A KV 1 with reinforced armour, captured and reused probably by the 1. Panzerdivision. The shortage of equipment forced the Germans to use anything available; but in the case of the T 34 and KV 1 this was done willingly.

A T 34/76 model 41 (or A) recovered by the Germans. The unit is unknown. Even though it was very much appreciated by the troops, the use of modern Soviet equipment posed a great problem to the maintenance units because of the lack of spare parts. There were also problems for the Panzerjäger because of the frequent confusion.

T-34 AND SOVIET MATILDA II

A T 34/76 1941 model. This vehicle was in every way superior to those that the Germans were able to deploy in their Panzerdivisionen. *'Za Rodinu!'* in red on the turret is a patriotic slogan meaning 'For the Fatherland'.

A T 34/76 1941 model destroyed in the 11. Panzerdivision sector. This vehicle was perfectly adapted to the Russian terrain and climate. The wide track reduced the risk of sinking up to the hull in soft ground
The yellow square insignia with a figure 2 is repeated on the other side of the turret, as well as under the gun, where the 2 is without its square.

A Matilda II used by the Soviets on the Moscow front during the winter of 1941-1942. The Matilda often bore technical data, in stencil form, in English. The mid-green British camouflage was left such as it was, only a coat of white was applied over it.

LIGHT AND MEDIUM SOVIET TANKS, SPRING 1941

A T-60 during the first weeks of combat. This type of light tank, derived from an amphibious vehicle, was used essentially for reconnaissance. Its road speed of 44 kph (27 mph) was not always enough to shelter from enemy fire and its armour was very insufficient, as was its armament: a single 20mm gun. In spite of that, about 6 000 T-60s were built.
Later it would be a chassis for the famous Stalin organs.

A T-34 1941 model. The finish of these tanks was not yet perfect, rationalisation would bring that about later. The Soviets simplified their manufacture as much as possible to allow for mass production. The production cost of the T-34 and KV-1 tanks would thus be halved. The main fault of the T-34, apart from its very basic finish, was the absence of a radio in the majority of tanks. Communication was therefore carried out with the aid of small flags, which often encouraged the crews to close the turret during the action and to charge forward, with the destruction of the tank being the very frequent outcome.

A T-34 1940 model. First of the large T-34 family, it was to be the most significant surprise for the Germans during the first months of the conflict. Compared to the Panzers, the T-34 was superior in every domain, except for the absence of a radio. Its very robust Diesel engine made on- board fires a very rare occurrence. Its Christie track wheels and its very wide track meant it was perfectly adapted to difficult terrain.

LIGHT AND MEDIUM SOVIET TANKS, SPRING 1941

A BT-5 from an unknown Soviet unit, at the beginning of the hostilities. Because of its high road speed and its 45mm gun capable of destroying practically all the Panzers deployed at the time, the BT was, theoretically at least, superior to many German tanks. But the armour of the BT-5 was too weak and certainly too fragile: in June 1941 its availability rate was very low.

A BT-7 probably belonging to the 5th Tanki Division. This tank was destroyed in Lithuania 22nd June 1941. The BT-7 differed from the BT-5 in that it had a sloping turret, which offered a certain protection against bullets, thereby compensating for the weakness of the armour. That said, the BT-7 was an insufficiently protected tank, which easily caught fire when it was hit.

A T-26B captured and reused by the Stu. Brig. 203, in the Kiev region, August 1941. The black figures on the front left of the tank (see detail), which are of Soviet origin, are possibly a registration or unit number. The T-26 was probably the most common in the Red Army inventory in June 1941 although, like all old Soviet tanks, they were very badly maintained, which meant their availability rate was deplorably low; less than 30%.

SOVIET AFVs

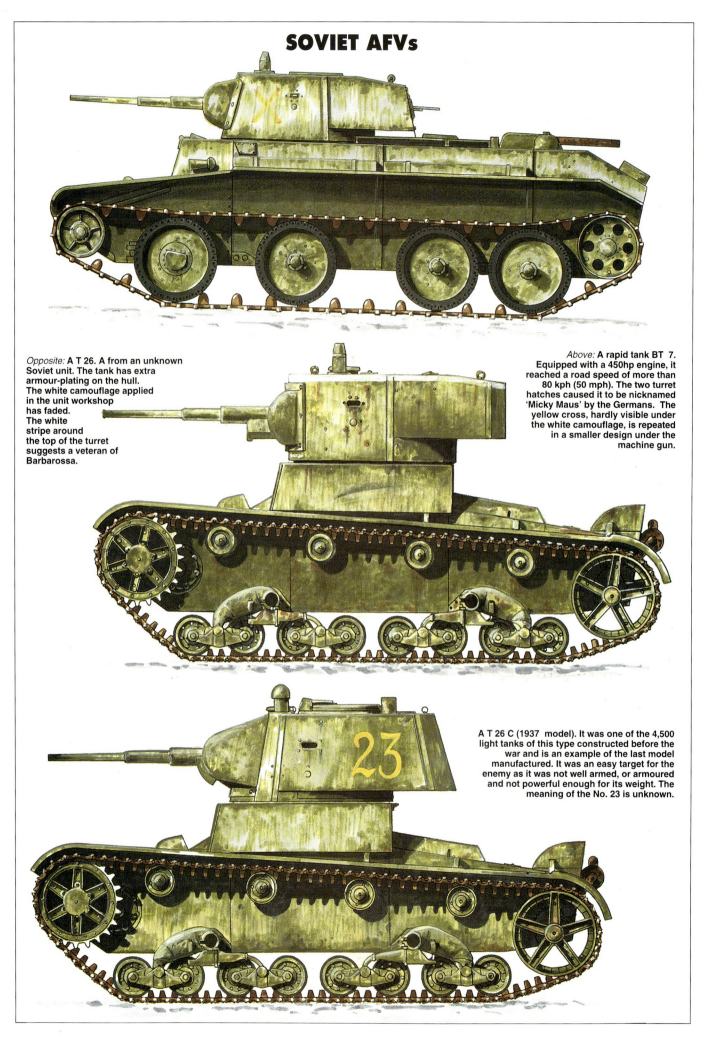

Above: **A rapid tank BT 7.** Equipped with a 450hp engine, it reached a road speed of more than 80 kph (50 mph). The two turret hatches caused it to be nicknamed 'Micky Maus' by the Germans. The yellow cross, hardly visible under the white camouflage, is repeated in a smaller design under the machine gun.

Opposite: **A T 26. A** from an unknown Soviet unit. The tank has extra armour-plating on the hull. The white camouflage applied in the unit workshop has faded. The white stripe around the top of the turret suggests a veteran of Barbarossa.

A T 26 C (1937 model). It was one of the 4,500 light tanks of this type constructed before the war and is an example of the last model manufactured. It was an easy target for the enemy as it was not well armed, or armoured and not powerful enough for its weight. The meaning of the No. 23 is unknown.

SOVIET AFVs

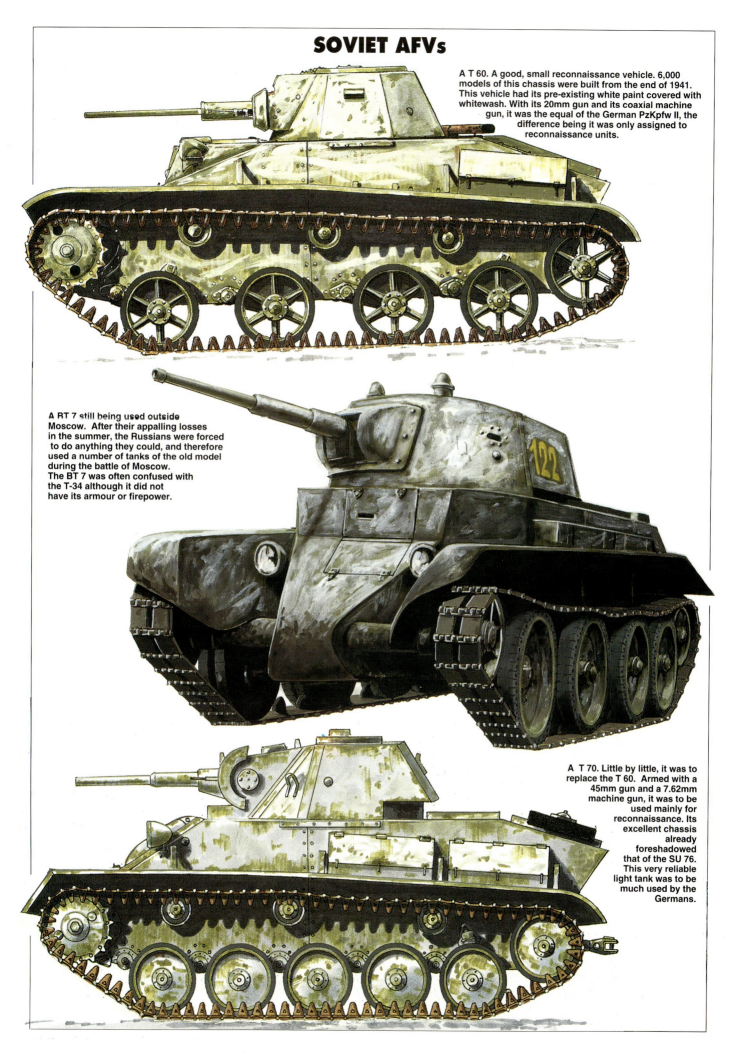

A T 60. A good, small reconnaissance vehicle. 6,000 models of this chassis were built from the end of 1941. This vehicle had its pre-existing white paint covered with whitewash. With its 20mm gun and its coaxial machine gun, it was the equal of the German PzKpfw II, the difference being it was only assigned to reconnaissance units.

A BT 7 still being used outside Moscow. After their appalling losses in the summer, the Russians were forced to do anything they could, and therefore used a number of tanks of the old model during the battle of Moscow. The BT 7 was often confused with the T-34 although it did not have its armour or firepower.

A T 70. Little by little, it was to replace the T 60. Armed with a 45mm gun and a 7.62mm machine gun, it was to be used mainly for reconnaissance. Its excellent chassis already foreshadowed that of the SU 76. This very reliable light tank was to be much used by the Germans.

SOVIET TANKS, 1941-42

A Valentine Mk III used by the Soviets. This tank was one of the 2 690 Valentines delivered to the Soviet Union by the Anglo-Canadians from October 1941 to 1943. The British green is still visible under the whitewash.

A KV 1 1940 model of the 1st battalion, 116th armoured brigade, during the winter of 1941/1942. The unit insignia is painted in yellow on a green background. A white camouflage was added over this.

A KV 1 1941 model. Still feared by the Germans because it outclassed all the Panzers of that period as much for its armament as for its armour. It is presumed that the figure or letter O was painted in red on the white camouflage. It is repeated at the rear of the turret.

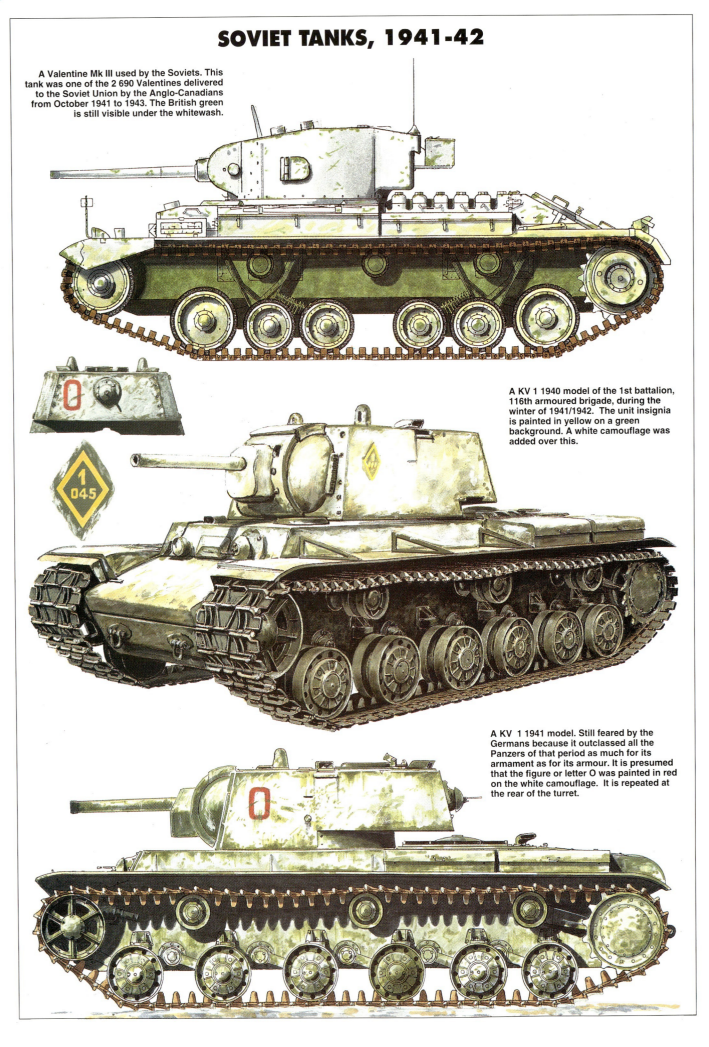

HEAVY SOVIET TANKS, SPRING 1941

T-35 of the 8th Soviet army corps (tactical sign on the rear turret). With five turrets and ten crewmen, the T-35 was more of a terrestrial battleship than an armoured vehicle. Armed with a 76.2mm gun fed by 96 shells, two 45mm guns with 220 shells and no less than 10,000 rounds for its five machine guns, the T-35 had the combined firepower of one Panzer IV and two Panzer III. On their own admission, the Germans never managed to destroy one of these monsters. All of them were abandoned due to mechanical failure or shortage of petrol.

A KV-2, the most impressive tank in the Soviet arsenal in June 1941. Its armour and its 152mm gun made it practically invincible. Only the 88mm gun, as was always the case, could destroy the KV-2. When no other gun of this type was available only machine gun fire through the vision slits or aimed at the turret ring could cause any damage, as well as lighted Jerrycans which were thrown at the tanks. Having said that, the very heavy KV-2 was often its own enemy and got stuck easily in difficult terrain.

A T-28 from an unknown unit, probably in the Baltic countries. Despite its imposing size, the T-28 was not a heavy but a medium tank. It was badly armoured, slow and fitted with poor optical sights and therefore did not represent a great danger for the Panzer II and IV. Its 76.2mm gun and its flexible suspension were not enough to make up for such handicaps.

HEAVY SOVIET TANKS AND ARMOURED CARS, 1941

KV-1 1940 model, without supplementary armour. This heavy Soviet tank was a very painful surprise for the Germans. The Panzer IV, all 20 tonnes of it, was half the weight of the KV-1, and yet it was the heaviest tank that the Germans were able to deploy. Well armed and well protected, very often supplied with a radio, the KV-1 was the source of a lot of worry for the Panzer-Divisionen which were not expecting to encounter such a vehicle. Only the ubiquitous 88mm gun proved itself capable of stopping them.

A BA-10 during the Summer of 1941 fighting. This excellent armoured car was both well armed and very much at ease on all types of terrain. Its 45mm gun, superior to the German 3.7 cm guns, was equal to the 5 cm guns in effectiveness. At the rear, the dual wheel carriage could be fitted with a small track which made off-road driving easier. The Germans would reuse the BA-10 as much as possible.

A KV-1 1940 model with extra armour riveted on. This tank had very few worthy rivals within the Panzerwaffe. The StuG III and the Pz IV had to get very near to it to destroy it and, in so doing, took a significant risk. In the Guari sector, in Estonia, on the road to Dunaburg-Pleiskau, two KV-1s of this type, with no inscription or insignia, spread a wave of panic for a while in the 6. Panzer-Division.

THE KLIMENTI VOROCHILOV-1A AND 1B

A KV 1 of the 116th Tankeibrigade, March 1942. The 1 figure indicates this unit's senior regiment while 045 is the brigade's tactical number. This lozenge-type marking later appeared in yellow paint, then after 1943, returned to white again.

KV 1 heavy tank of an unidentified unit. The name 'Tchapaeiv' stands for a famous revolutionary cavalry general. Another inscription has apparently been painted over on the turret side. Although it is fitted with a Type A turret, the chassis and wheels and tracks are more recent. This tank has also been retrofitted with the long-barrelled version of the 7.62mm gun.

KV 1B with additional bolted armour plates. The original tank is a KV 1 A. This would bring the gross weight to 47,5 tonnes. Thus the ratio is now of 11,6 hp per ton instead of 12,6 hp per ton previously. The main gun is the short barrelled 7.62mm.

1944

FRANCE

SOMUA S 35 TANKS AND PzKpfW IV

Panzerkampfwagen IV Ausf. H of the 3rd company of the I./Pz.Rgt. 130, Panzer-Lehr Division. Green camouflage on a sand background. Above: detail of the mudguard with the tactical sign of the tank units and the Panzer-Lehr sign.

0   1   2   3   4

Somua S 35 of the 6th company of the II./22. Pz.Rgt. (21. Pz.Div.), at the beginning of the Normandy campaign. The II. Abteilung should have been equipped with the Panther but it only received a few rather late.
Two companies were to be equipped with StuG III 40 G assault guns and the rest with PzKpfW IV Ausf. H. (below).

PzKpfW IV Ausf. H of the 6th company of the II./22. Pz.Rgt. (21. Pz.Div.), near Grandmesnil (Caen region), mid-August 1944. Classical green camouflage on sand applied on the spot, stencilled white numbers, no German cross.

MEDIUM GERMAN TANKS

A Panzer IV Ausf. H of the 1. SS-Panzerdivision 'Leibstandarte Adolf Hitler', II. Abteilung. This tank was the battle-horse of the Panzerwaffe throughout the conflict. Even though it was conceived on old lines, it was constantly improved and remained, with a good crew, a very dangerous adversary.

A PzKpfW IV Ausf. H of the 12. SS-Panzerdivision "Hitlerjugend". It belonged to the 7. Kompanie, II. Abteilung. The first battalion was equipped with Panthers. A particularity of this unit was the turret numbers: the platoon leader had a number finishing in 5 (715 for example). Followed next by 6, 7 and 8 (716, 717, 718). The numbers were very badly painted on the Zimmerit coating.

A Panther Ausf. A of the II./Panzer-Regiment 3, 2. Panzerdivision. This platoon leader's tank could be that of Leutnant Neffzern. After the crossing of the Seine, at the end of August 1944, the 2. Panzerdivision had only three tanks and three Jagdpanzer.

PANZERKAMPFWAGEN IV Ausf. H AND J

A Panzerkampfwagen IV Ausf. H from a company of the 9. SS-Pz.Div. 'Hohenstaufen'. The tank is painted in a three-colour camouflage, green and red-brown on a sand background. The absence of a number on the turret possibly resulted from a lack of time, although it was the case that tanks bore fewer and fewer tactical signs from spring 1944.

A Panzerkampfwagen IV Ausf. H of the 6th company of the II./2. SS-Pz.Rgt. ('Das Reich' division), in the Saint-Fromont-Saint Lô region, early July 1944. Here also, the camouflage is in three shades.

A PzKpfW IV Ausf. J of the 5th company of the II./12. SS-Pz.Rgt., 'Hitlerjugend' division. This tank, whose figures were painted by hand because of the lack of stencils, was that of Oberscharführer Willy Kretzschmar. Following mechanical problems, this tank was scuppered by its crew in the Falaise pocket, 20th August 1944.

GERMAN TIGER AND ROCKET-LAUNCHERS

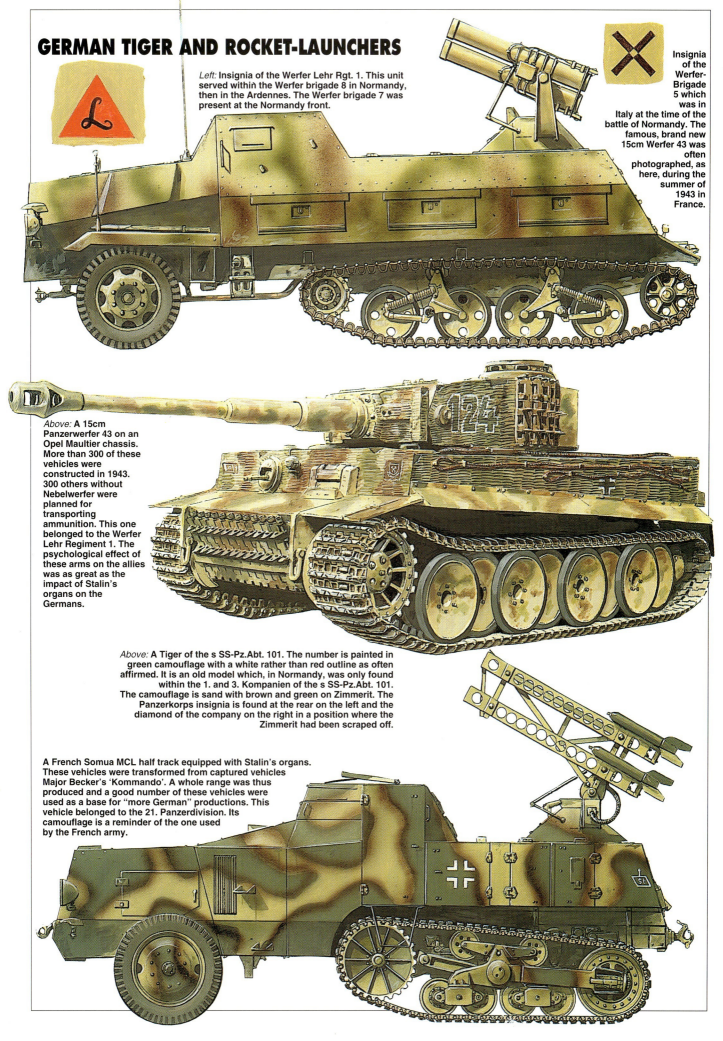

Left: Insignia of the Werfer Lehr Rgt. 1. This unit served within the Werfer brigade 8 in Normandy, then in the Ardennes. The Werfer brigade 7 was present at the Normandy front.

Insignia of the Werfer-Brigade 5 which was in Italy at the time of the battle of Normandy. The famous, brand new 15cm Werfer 43 was often photographed, as here, during the summer of 1943 in France.

Above: A 15cm Panzerwerfer 43 on an Opel Maultier chassis. More than 300 of these vehicles were constructed in 1943. 300 others without Nebelwerfer were planned for transporting ammunition. This one belonged to the Werfer Lehr Regiment 1. The psychological effect of these arms on the allies was as great as the impact of Stalin's organs on the Germans.

Above: A Tiger of the s SS-Pz.Abt. 101. The number is painted in green camouflage with a white rather than red outline as often affirmed. It is an old model which, in Normandy, was only found within the 1. and 3. Kompanien of the s SS-Pz.Abt. 101. The camouflage is sand with brown and green on Zimmerit. The Panzerkorps insignia is found at the rear on the left and the diamond of the company on the right in a position where the Zimmerit had been scraped off.

A French Somua MCL half track equipped with Stalin's organs. These vehicles were transformed from captured vehicles Major Becker's 'Kommando'. A whole range was thus produced and a good number of these vehicles were used as a base for "more German" productions. This vehicle belonged to the 21. Panzerdivision. Its camouflage is a reminder of the one used by the French army.

PANZERKAMPFWAGEN V PANTHER

A Panther Ausf. G of the
3rd company of the 12.
SS-Pz.Rgt., 'Hitlerjugend'
division (initially in the I.
SS-Panzer Korps),
captured in the
Caen region.

0   1   2   3   4

A Panther Ausf. G of the 1st
company of the 12. SS-Pz.Rgt.
This tank, whose commander
was Zugführer Dittrich, was hit
during an attack on Bretteville,
9th June 1944.

A Panther Ausf. A of the
3rd company of the I./2.
SS-Pz.Rgt., 'Das Reich'
division, seen in the Falaise
pocket. All the side *Schürzen*
have been ripped off, leaving
only the mounts.

PANZERKAMPFWAGEN V PANTHER

A Panther Ausf. A of the 2nd company of the I./6. Pz.Rgt. Originally in the 3. Pz.Div., this battalion was assigned to the Panzer-Lehr Division, 22nd January 1944.

0	1	2	3	4

A Jagdpanther of the 2nd company of the schwerer Panzerjäger-Abteilung 654, the only company having these tank destroyers (12 of them) on the Normandy front. On 27th June 1944, the 2./s.Pz.Jg.Abt. 654 was under the command of the Weidinger group (Panzer-Lehr Division), in the Mondrainville-Grainville-Rauray region.

A Panther Ausf. G of the 1st company of the I./9. SS-Pz.Rgt., 'Hohenstaufen' division. This tank was destroyed at Saint-André-sur-Orne on 22nd July 1944.

PANZERKAMPFWAGEN VI TIGER Ausf. E

The I. SS-Pz.Kps. sign.

A Tiger I Ausf. E of the s. SS-Pz.Abt. 101. This vehicle, bearing the number 007, was the tank in which Hauptsturmführer (captain) Michael Wittmann and his crew were killed, 8th August 1944, approximately 1 km north of Cintheaux. It is supposed that Wittmann's Tiger, as well as several others, were destroyed that day by Firefly Shermans from A Squadron, 1st Northamptonshire Yeomanry (33rd Independent Armoured Brigade).

A Tiger I of the 3rd company of the s.SS-Panzer-Abteilung 101 in August 1944 in the Caen region. This tank is seen on the left of the Panther '308' of the 3rd company of the 12.SS-Pz.Div. 'Hitlerjugend', on a photo showing equipment captured by the British.

A Tiger I of the 2nd company of the s.SS-Panzer-Abteilung 102, tank commander Ustuf. Walter Schroif, Normandy, August 1944. Under the command of SS-Sturmbahnführer Weiz, the battalion destroyed more than 227 tanks, 28 antitank guns, 19 heavy armoured vehicles, 4 armoured reconnaissance vehicles and 35 trucks.

PANZERKAMPFWAGEN VI TIGER Ausf.E AND TIGER II

A Tiger I Ausf. E of the s.Pz.Abt. 503. Commanded by Feldwebel Sachs, the '313', on the morning of the 11th July 1944, took part in the destruction of 11 Shermans and 5 antitank guns during a counter-attack north of Colombelles. However, on the 18th July, because of the violent aerial bombing preceding operation Goodwood, the '313' rolled over onto its turret, killing two crewmen.

A Tiger II of the 1st company of the s.Panzer-Abteilung 503. This company's Königstigers were the only ones to fight effectively in Normandy.
Right: detail of the rear turret panel, with the repetition of the number.

A Tiger II of the 3rd company of the s.Panzer-Abteilung 503. This company, en route to Normandy via Paris, was attacked 12th August between Sézanne and Esterney by 5 thunderbolts. One of the 5 Tiger IIs in the convoy, Lieutenant von Rosen's '311', was abandoned. Subsequently the company was wiped out, the last tank (Lt. Rambow) was scuppered in the Amiens region.

Detail of the turret of the Tiger I No. 122 (2nd tank, 2nd section of the 1st company) of s.SS-Pz.Abt. 101. The number in green camouflage outlined in white is repeated on the *'Rommelkist'* (stowage bin at the rear of the turret). The spare track links were sometimes camouflaged. When they were changed, if they had not been used, sometimes marks of paint were left, or otherwise they were rusty due to previous use, as we can see here.

101. s.SS-Pz.Abt.

A Tiger I of the initial model (rubber tyre wheels) of the 101. s.SS-Pz.Abt. This tank, numerically the last in the battalion, was damaged and abandoned at Roncey, 27th June. Subsequently it was subjected to trials by the British. The Durham Light Infantry claimed responsibility for its destruction, although no holes are visible on this tank. The shape of the figure 4 is common to this unit's three companies.

Example of the forward glacis of tanks of the 1. Kp. of the 101. s.SS-Pz.Abt. The trapezium sign of the tank units was sometimes painted on Zimmerit. The shield was a pointed shape.

Example of the forward glacis of tanks of the 2. Kp. of the 101; s.SS-Pz.Abt. Here the shield appears on the front right of the tank.

Example of the forward glacis of the 3; Kp. in the 101. s.SS-Pz.Abt. In the majority of cases, the badge of the I. SS-Panzer Korps was painted on a black background.

The insignia of the I. SS-Panzer Korps. The shield had a pointed or rounded base, depending on the tank.

Detail of the Tiger I No. 006, 2nd tank of the Stabskompanie of the 101. s.SS-Pz.Abt.

The Tiger I No. 205 was the tank of Obersturmführer Wittmann, commander of the 2nd company, 101 s.SS-Pz.Abt.

Detail of the number painted on the rear turret stowage bin of the last tank of the 1st section, 3rd company of the 101. s.SS-Pz.Abt. The shape of the figures is typical.

Tiger I of the commander of the
2nd platoon, 2nd company
of the s.SS-Pz.Abt. 102.
The number, simply
outlined on the
background
camouflage, is
repeated on the
'Rommelkiste', here
in black figures
outlined in white.
No. 221,
commanded by
Hauptsturmführer
Lindemann, was to be
the first tank lost by the
battalion.

102. s.SS-Pz.Abt.

Detail of the forward glacis of a
tank from the 102. s.SS-Pz.Abt.,
showing the position of the rune
of the II. SS-Panzer Korps as well
as its unexpected pink colour.

503. s.Heeres Pz.Abt.

The Tiger II of Leutnant Piepgras,
commander of the 2nd platoon, 1st company
of the s.Heeres Pz.Abt. 503. This tank was
one of those lost in combat. The officer and
his crew managed to escape. Leutnant
Piepgras later fought in Hungary and
survived the war.

The insignia of the 503.
s.Heeres Pz.Abt.was
practically never painted
on the tanks, in any case
not in Normandy.

This Porsche turret of a Tiger II illustrates
an unconfirmed possibility of the
presence of 'simple' camouflage in
Normandy. The absence of a number is
due, either to the new camouflage of the
tank after a number of superficial hits or,
as was often the case at this time, it was
the result of a last minute delivery
forbidding the painting of a number. In
both cases however, the lack of time
remains the most obvious cause.

101. s.SS-Pz.Abt.

This 20 mm quadruple 'Flakvierling' on a Panzer IV chassis belongs to the Flak Zug (AA platoon) of s.SS-Panzer-Abteilung 101 (formation sign on the right hand side front mudguard). Each heavy tank battalion had such a unit equipped with this AFV.

A Tiger I, No 224, of s.SS-Pz.Abt.102. This is Uscha. Oberhaber's machine, who scored three kills on 20 July 1944. He destroyed a few more before the end of the war, which he survived. The turret side number is outlined in white on the camouflage background, whereas it is outlined in black on the *'Rommelkist'*. The 2. Panzerkorps sign, here shown on the hull rear, was not systematically painted on the unit's tanks.

102. s.SS-Pz.Abt.

The 18 tonnes half tracked prime mover and recovery vehicle had 250 hp. It was used for towing disabled Tigers in s. SS-Pz.Abt. 102 (whose sign is painted on the left hand side mudguard), three tractors being necessary to move the armoured monsters. The s.Pz.Abt. 503's Tiger IIs required Bergepanthers for their recovery.

SUMMER 1944

This Tiger I, No 112 of s. SS-Pz.Abt. 101, is one of the German tanks destroyed at Villers-Bocage. The turret numbers appear in outline on the camouflage pattern.

503. s.Heeres Pz.Abt.

Tiger I No 224 of s.Pz.Abt. 503, black numbers outlined in white. This unit's 2. Kompanie was the only one to play an active role in the Normandy fighting. Camouflage patterns were not as 'heavy' as in the other two Tiger heavy battalions in this theatre of operations.

iger II, No 321 of eformed 3. panie, s.Pz.Abt. This unit's nks never got a ce to prove worth, as they rey to Allied er-bombers East aris on their way e Normandy front.

THE MODIFIED 38 H IN NORMANDY

A Selbsfahrlafette 7.5 cm-Pak 40 auf Fahrgestell-Panzerkampfwagen 38 H (f) of the 21. Panzer Division in Normandy, June 1944. It belonged to the Sturmgeschütz Abteilung 200. 48 machines were built, all assigned to the 21. Panzer.

A Grosser Funk und Befehlpanzer 38 H (f). Only 24 were built. Panzer-Artillerie Regiment 155 (21. Panzerdivision) was certainly equipped with these artillery observation vehicles.

A 10.5 cm - the FH 18/40 auf Geschützwagen 38 H (f) of the Panzer-Artillerie Regiment 155 of the 21. Panzerdivision, in Normandy at the time of the landings. Some of these SPGs served within the Sturmgeschütz-Abteilung 200.

1   2   3   4m

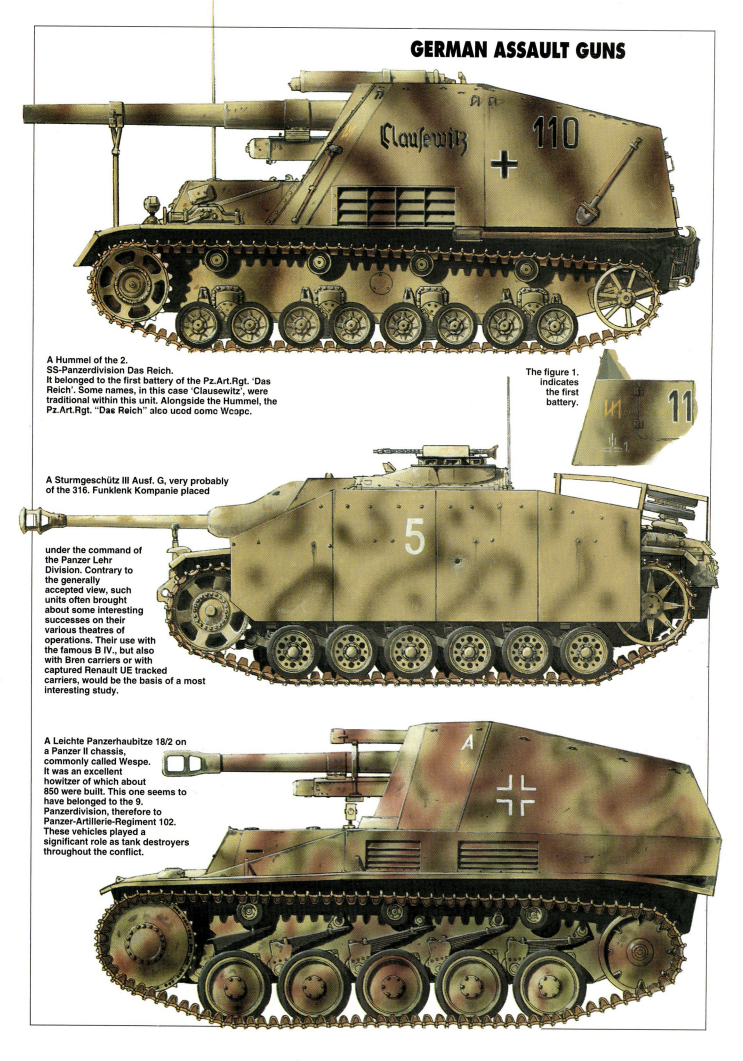

A Hummel of the 2. SS-Panzerdivision Das Reich. It belonged to the first battery of the Pz.Art.Rgt. 'Das Reich'. Some names, in this case 'Clausewitz', were traditional within this unit. Alongside the Hummel, the Pz.Art.Rgt. "Das Reich" also used some Wespe.

The figure 1. indicates the first battery.

A Sturmgeschütz III Ausf. G, very probably of the 316. Funklenk Kompanie placed under the command of the Panzer Lehr Division. Contrary to the generally accepted view, such units often brought about some interesting successes on their various theatres of operations. Their use with the famous B IV., but also with Bren carriers or with captured Renault UE tracked carriers, would be the basis of a most interesting study.

A Leichte Panzerhaubitze 18/2 on a Panzer II chassis, commonly called Wespe. It was an excellent howitzer of which about 850 were built. This one seems to have belonged to the 9. Panzerdivision, therefore to Panzer-Artillerie-Regiment 102. These vehicles played a significant role as tank destroyers throughout the conflict.

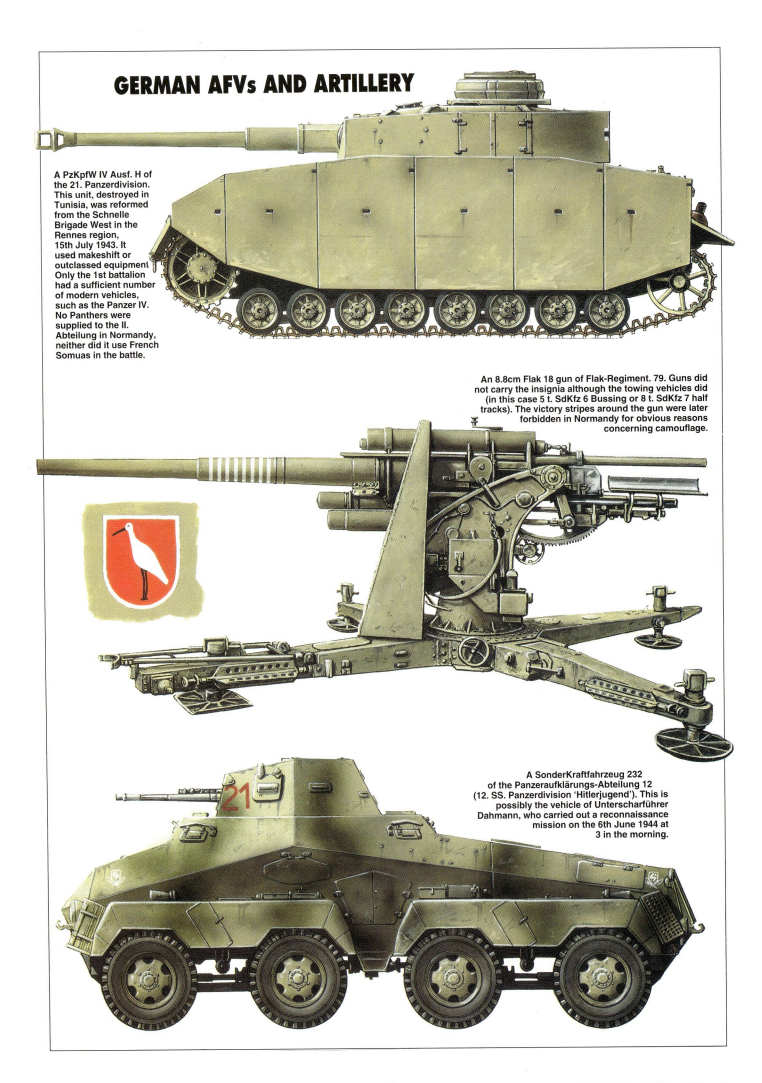

GERMAN AFVs AND ARTILLERY

A PzKpfW IV Ausf. H of the 21. Panzerdivision. This unit, destroyed in Tunisia, was reformed from the Schnelle Brigade West in the Rennes region, 15th July 1943. It used makeshift or outclassed equipment Only the 1st battalion had a sufficient number of modern vehicles, such as the Panzer IV. No Panthers were supplied to the II. Abteilung in Normandy, neither did it use French Somuas in the battle.

An 8.8cm Flak 18 gun of Flak-Regiment. 79. Guns did not carry the insignia although the towing vehicles did (in this case 5 t. SdKfz 6 Bussing or 8 t. SdKfz 7 half tracks). The victory stripes around the gun were later forbidden in Normandy for obvious reasons concerning camouflage.

A SonderKraftfahrzeug 232 of the Panzeraufklärungs-Abteilung 12 (12. SS. Panzerdivision 'Hitlerjugend'). This is possibly the vehicle of Unterscharführer Dahmann, who carried out a reconnaissance mission on the 6th June 1944 at 3 in the morning.

STURMGESCHÜTZ III AND STURMHAUBITZE H 42

A StuG III 40 of the 341. Sturmgeschützbrigade, which had its first engagement 31st July 1944 in the Avranches-Brécey region. Twice reformed, this unit lost all its assault guns during allied air attacks towards the end of the battle of Normandy. On the vehicle shown, the rear side armour plate had been retrieved from another tank.

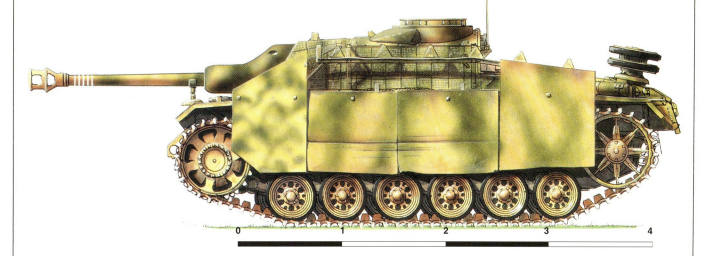

A StuG III 40 of the II./22. Pz.Rgt. (21. Pz.Div.). Two companies of Sturmgeschütze were engaged alongside the I. and II. Panzer Abteilungen, 12. SS 'Hitlerjugend' Division, during fighting in the Grainville-Marcelet-Mouen zone, 26th June 1944.

A StuH 42 (SdKfz. 142/2) of the 2nd company of the Sturmgeschützbrigade 394, seen during fighting in the region of Vire. The vehicle is equipped with a 10.5cm L 28 howitzer.

JAGDPANZER IV AND STURMGESCHÜTZ IV

A Jagdpanzer IV Ausf. F (SdKfz 162) of the 1st company SS-Panzerjäger-Abteilung 12. during fighting in the Cagny-Vimont region, 17th-18th July 1944. The first company, under the command of Obersturmführer Georg Hurdelbrink, had just arrived at the theatre of operations, the 2nd and 3rd were to rejoin them later. On August 10th, on hill 111 north-west of Rouvres, Hurdelbrink alone destroyed 11 tanks, and 7 more were destroyed by one of his subordinates, Oberscharführer Rudolf Roy.

```
0        1        2        3        4
```

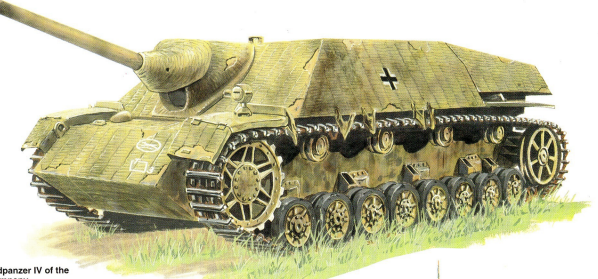

A Jagdpanzer IV of the 3rd company, 228.Panzerjäger Abteilung, 116. Pz.Div., July 1944. The vehicle, painted in sand, was re-sprayed all over with a greenish coat, sand yellow being too light against the greenery of Normandy.

A Sturmgeschütz IV, probably in the 394. StuG. Brigade, Vire region. On 6th August 1944, its 3rd battery destroyed 26 Shermans and freed an infantry battalion which had just been captured. Note the A indicating the battery, a paradox compared to the '211' of the 2. Kp. *(see the Sturmhaubitze 42, p. 101)*.

AMPHIBIOUS TANKS

An M3 A3 light tank of the 13/18th Hussars at Brèche d'Hermanville on Sword beach, the morning of 6th June 1944. The vehicle is equipped with two air shafts allowing air into the engine and the exhaust. Allied standard light tanks, the M3, A3 or M5, were totally surpassed by 1944 with their 37mm gun and light armour.

T 213758

A Sherman Duplex Drive of the 10th Canadian Armoured Regiment, which landed on 'Nan', one of the sectors of Juno beach. This unit played a part in the support of the Queen's Own Rifles of Canada and the North Shore Regiment.

'Cannon Ball' was an M4 Sherman of the 741st Tank Battalion which landed on Omaha beach along with the first infantry assault waves. Practically all the amphibious Sherman DDs of this unit were lost at sea, models equipped with a wading device like this one did not fare much better as they were almost all destroyed, one by one, by German antitank artillery.

CANNON BALL 2 USA 3066192

AMERICAN AND BRITISH TANKS

A Sherman M4 A3, 75mm, of H. Co, 66th Armored Regiment, 2nd US Armored Division. This was one of the first tanks to land on D day. The vehicle is splashed from top to bottom with sandy water. On top of the turret it carries a white star in a white circle. The white circle is as wide as the access hatch and is situated to the left of it.

A Cromwell of the 11th British Armoured Division in the Hérouvillette region, 14th June 1944. The white marks to the right of the gun and under the registration number on the lower front armour are the remains of transfers stating the dimensions and weight of the vehicles boarded onto the LCTs.

Detail of the forward part of the 'Cromwell' (with the turret) and the ship loading specification transfer, on the top right.

A Cromwell of the Sharpshooters, (4th County of London Yeomanry, 22nd Brigade), 12th June 1944, near Villers-Bocage. This tank was to be destroyed the following day during the fighting for Villers-Bocage against Wittmann and his Tigers.

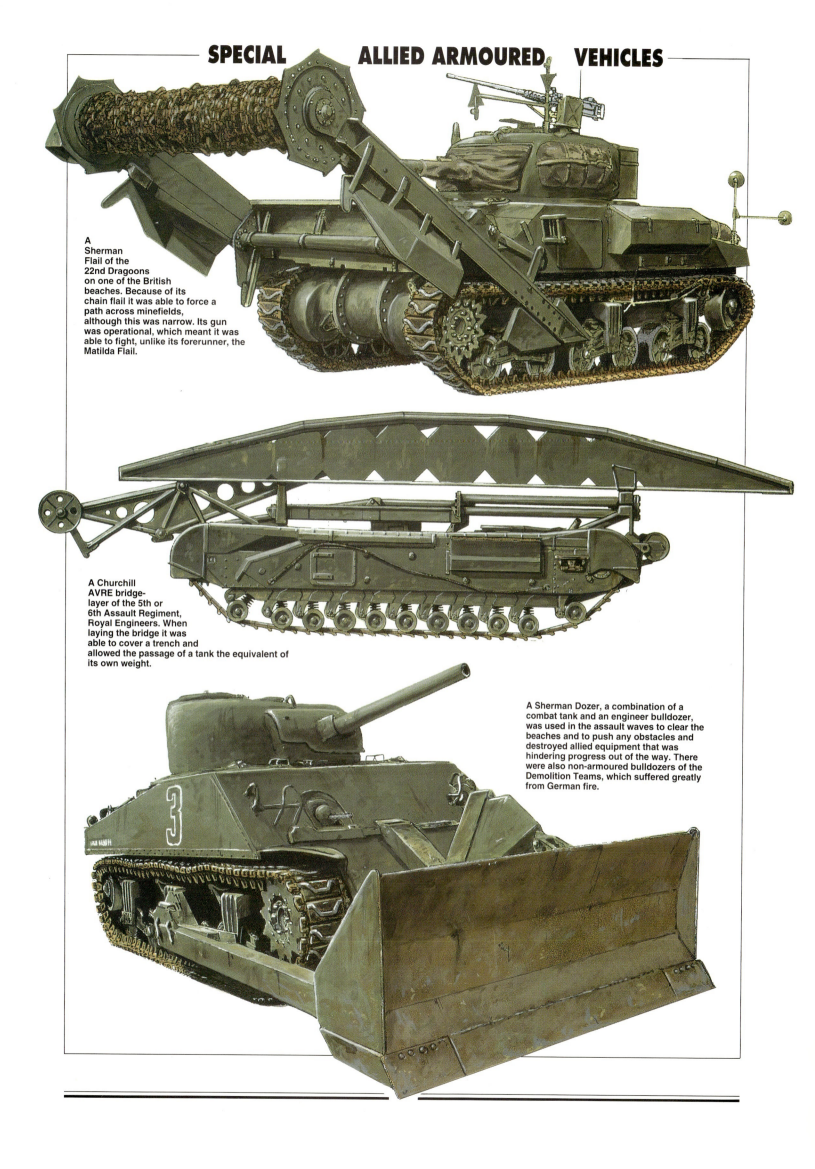

SPECIAL ALLIED ARMOURED VEHICLES

A Sherman Flail of the 22nd Dragoons on one of the British beaches. Because of its chain flail it was able to force a path across minefields, although this was narrow. Its gun was operational, which meant it was able to fight, unlike its forerunner, the Matilda Flail.

A Churchill AVRE bridge-layer of the 5th or 6th Assault Regiment, Royal Engineers. When laying the bridge it was able to cover a trench and allowed the passage of a tank the equivalent of its own weight.

A Sherman Dozer, a combination of a combat tank and an engineer bulldozer, was used in the assault waves to clear the beaches and to push any obstacles and destroyed allied equipment that was hindering progress out of the way. There were also non-armoured bulldozers of the Demolition Teams, which suffered greatly from German fire.

DUKW AND SUPPORT FIRE TANKS

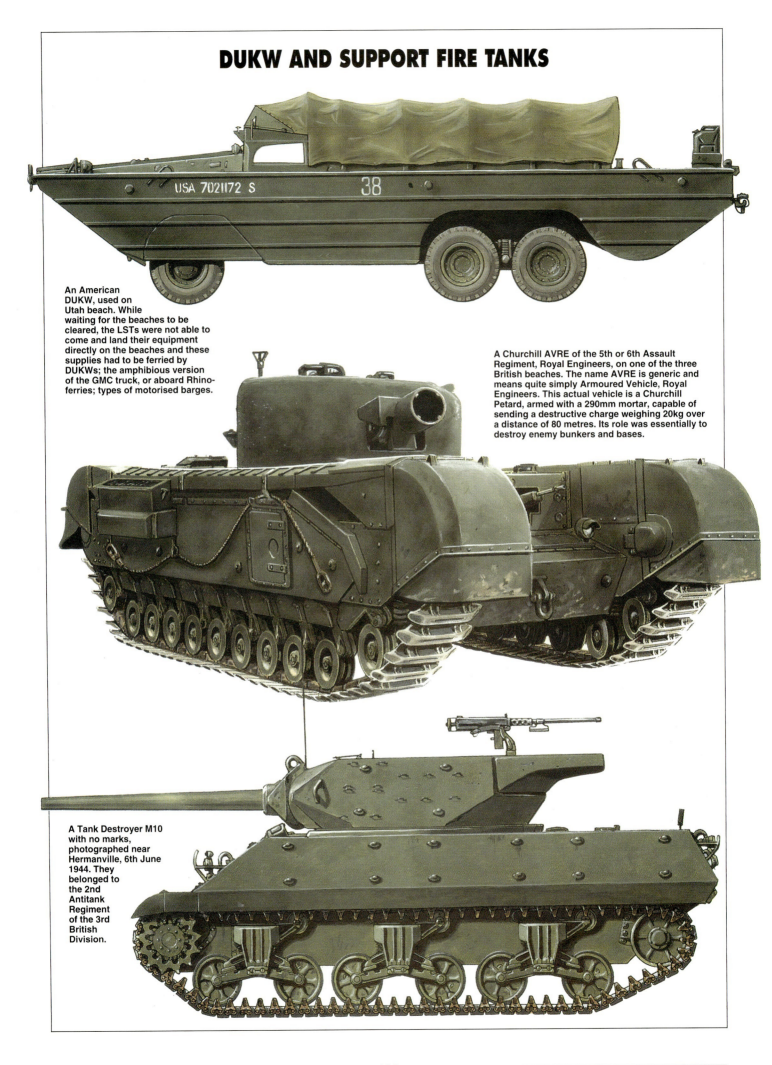

An American DUKW, used on Utah beach. While waiting for the beaches to be cleared, the LSTs were not able to come and land their equipment directly on the beaches and these supplies had to be ferried by DUKWs; the amphibious version of the GMC truck, or aboard Rhino-ferries; types of motorised barges.

A Churchill AVRE of the 5th or 6th Assault Regiment, Royal Engineers, on one of the three British beaches. The name AVRE is generic and means quite simply Armoured Vehicle, Royal Engineers. This actual vehicle is a Churchill Petard, armed with a 290mm mortar, capable of sending a destructive charge weighing 20kg over a distance of 80 metres. Its role was essentially to destroy enemy bunkers and bases.

A Tank Destroyer M10 with no marks, photographed near Hermanville, 6th June 1944. They belonged to the 2nd Antitank Regiment of the 3rd British Division.

BRITISH TANKS, CHURCHILL, CROMWELL AND CHALLENGER

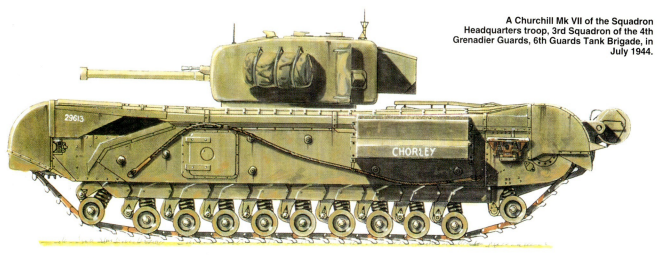

A Churchill Mk VII of the Squadron Headquarters troop, 3rd Squadron of the 4th Grenadier Guards, 6th Guards Tank Brigade, in July 1944.

Cromwell number T 187740 of the 11th Armoured Division, 8th corps, 14th June 1944 in the Hérouvillette region. The vehicle carries traces of transfers.

Below: Challenger of the 11th Armoured Division, Flers, 17th July 1944. Because of the triangle, it is supposed that it belonged to an A squadron. There were very few Challengers used in Normandy. The 17 pounder gun, which fired APDS ammunition (Armour Piercing Discarding Sabot), was easily the most formidable arm used on the battlefield, even compared to the Tiger II gun. Only its armour allowed the Tiger to fight, from a distance, opposite tanks equipped with such a formidable gun.

Rear view of the Challenger.

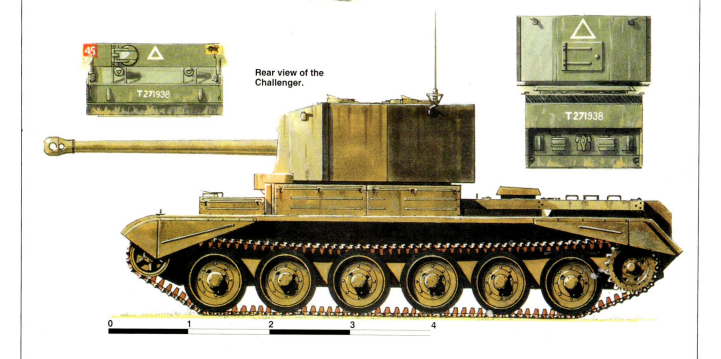

BRITISH TANKS, SHERMAN FIREFLY AND M4 A3, ACHILLES

PL 53

A Sherman Firefly of the 24th Lancers (Polish 1st Armoured Division) in the area of Arromanches, 2nd August 1944, at the time of its landing.

Detail of the inscription on the hull sides: *THIS VEHICLE IS FILLED WITH ANTIFREEZE 1/2 2/3 AND MUST NOT BE DRAINED.*

An Achilles, British version of the American M-10 Tank Destroyer. The difference being that the Achilles was equipped with the fearsome 17 pounder gun. This tank belonged to the 91st Antitank Regiment, Royal Artillery, directly attached to the 8t Corps HQ.

A Sherman M4 A3 of the HQ of the 23rd Hussars, 29th Armoured Brigade, 11th British Armoured Division, in the Saint-Manvieu region.

T147852

M3 A5 Stuart 'Concrete' from the C Company of an unidentified American unit. Later, the lower side plates would either be lost or removed.

A Sherman M4 A1 from an unidentified American unit. The tank bears the name 'Sherry' on the sides. The white stars had already been painted over.

A Canadian Sherman Firefly from B Coy., Canadian 27th

Armoured Regiment in the Buron region, 7th June 1944. This tank, along with 27 others, was destroyed by Pz. IVs of the 5th and 6th companies of the Panzer-Regiment 12 (12th SS 'Hitlerjugend' Division). The losses in this sector were very heavy on both sides.

AMERICAN AND BRITISH TANKS

A Cromwell from the British 11th Armoured Division, 17th July 1944 at Flers. The inscriptions and figures were added with a brush, probably the first names of the driver's or gunner's girlfriends.

A Sherman M4 A1 of C company, 67th Armored Regiment, 2nd US Armored Division, equipped with a 76mm gun. This tank, whose gun had not yet experienced combat gave rise to only a few criticisms from the American crews during the first days of the campaign. Three hundred tanks of this type took part in the invasion.

Sherman M4 A3 from H company, 66th Armored Regiment, 2nd US Armored Division *(also see on page 104)*, later in the campaign. The numbers and letters have disappeared. Later, this tank would be re-covered with brown streaks of camouflage.

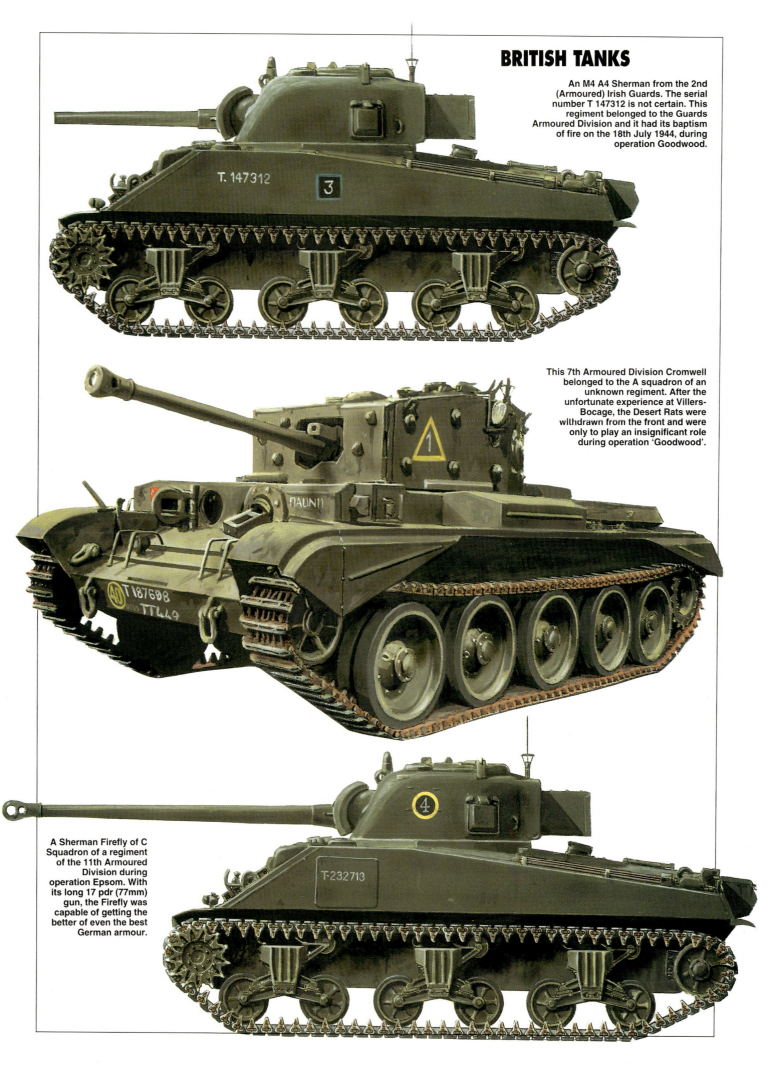

BRITISH TANKS

An M4 A4 Sherman from the 2nd (Armoured) Irish Guards. The serial number T 147312 is not certain. This regiment belonged to the Guards Armoured Division and it had its baptism of fire on the 18th July 1944, during operation Goodwood.

This 7th Armoured Division Cromwell belonged to the A squadron of an unknown regiment. After the unfortunate experience at Villers-Bocage, the Desert Rats were withdrawn from the front and were only to play an insignificant role during operation 'Goodwood'.

A Sherman Firefly of C Squadron of a regiment of the 11th Armoured Division during operation Epsom. With its long 17 pdr (77mm) gun, the Firefly was capable of getting the better of even the best German armour.

Above:
An M4A3, armed with a 76mm gun without muzzle brake. These tanks did not really please the troops at the beginning of their career, but this prejudice was short-lived. These tanks equipped the TD Battalions alongside the M10s and M36s. The 7 is the number of the tank within the company.

Opposite: An M4 Sherman of the 32nd Tank Battalion (3rd US Armored Division). This unit took part in the difficult advance towards Saint-Lô, crossing the Vire, at the beginning of the month of July. The white stars have been hastily covered over in order to make them less visible.

An M4A3 from an unknown American unit. The crew put dirt on the original olive Drab paint. The troops acted on their own initiative to try to improve their tanks: a more effective camouflage, the addition of sandbags for protection and so on.

Three Shermans from the 2e RC (2e régiment de cuirassiers - armoured regiment), a unit answering to General Sudre's Combat Command (CC 1), itself controlled by General Montsabert, the commanding officer of the 3rd DIA (Division d'Infanterie Algerienne - Algerian infantry division). Consolidated within the Groupement du Vigier, the rest of the French 1st Armoured Division (1ere Division Blindée Française) was engaged in the Rhone valley while Combat Command 1, along with the 3rd DIA, liberated Marseille. In 1944, 2e RC tanks were given the names of French towns such as here: 'Valenciennes', 'Tours' and 'Fabert' (the latter was commissioned with the 2nd Squadron, 2nd Armoured Regiment).

An M4 Sherman from an unidentified unit, although belonging to the 4th US Armored Division, Pontaubault, end of July 1944. Here again the stars are painted over with a darker tone.

M-10 Tank Destroyer (TD) from the 823rd TD Battalion which supported the 30th US infantry division in fighting around Saint-Jean-de-Daye, 11th July 1944.

An M-10 Tank Destroyer (TD) of the 1er peloton de combat du 2e escadron de combat du Regiment Blindé de Fusiliers Marins. This tank was to be destroyed 12th August 1944 in the Alençon region, one of the first losses recorded by the French 2e DB.

SHERMAN FIREFLY AND SHERMAN M4 A3

Sherman M4 A3 in the 2e peloton, 3e escadron du 1er Régiment de chasseurs d'Afrique of the French 2e DB, destroyed 12th July 1944, near Alençon.

45

ILE DE FRANCE

This M4 A3 Sherman, armed with a 105mm gun, probably belonged to the 4th US Armored Division.

A Firefly of the Sharpshooters (4th County of London Yeomanry, 22nd Brigade), 7th Armoured Division, destroyed or abandoned at Villers-Bocage, 13th June 1944.

STUART M3 A3 AND M5 A1, SHERMAN M4 A3

M3 A3 light tank from the 1er Escadron de combat du 12e régiment de cuirassiers, French 2e Division Blindée, number 420462.

A Sherman M4 A3, 2nd platoon, C. Co, 8th Tank Battalion, 4th US Armored Division, in the region of Avranches. These tanks were later dabbed with mud and clay, covering the white stars, which were too easily spotted by the enemy.

The 1st Polish Armoured Division sign, depicts an XVIIth century Polish Winged Hussars helmet (heavy cavalry).

M5 A1 light tanks of the 24th Lancers,

10th Armoured Brigade, 1st Polish Armoured Division, August 1944, in the Falaise cauldron.

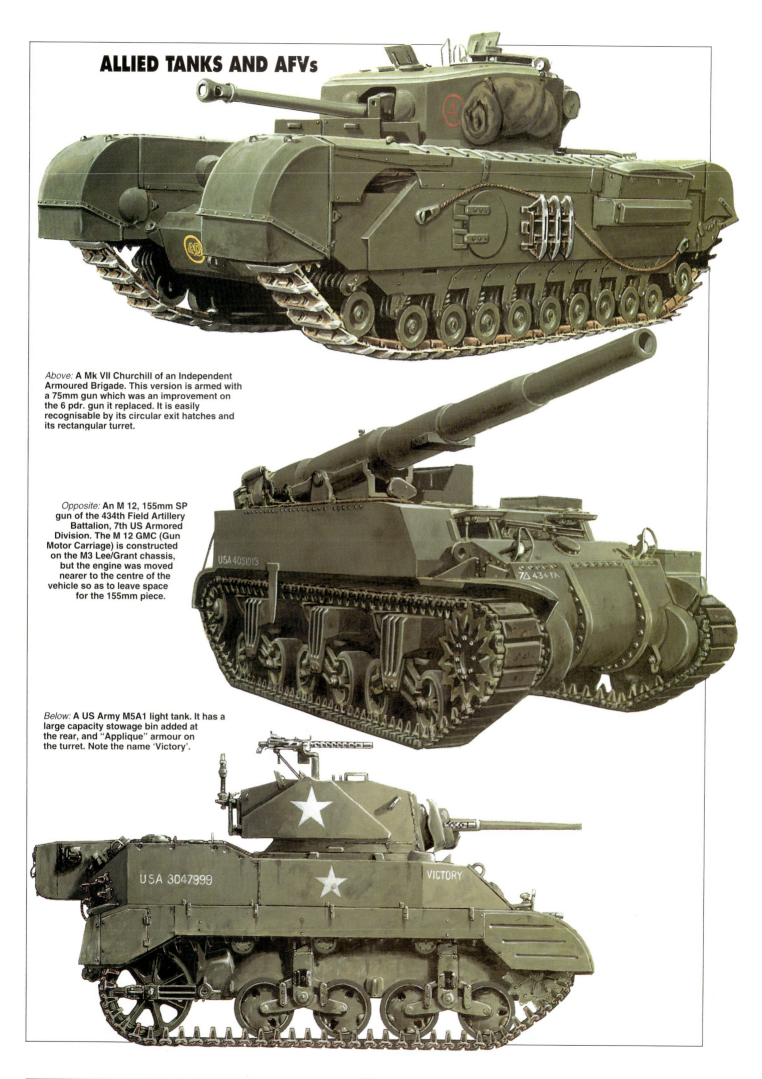

ALLIED TANKS AND AFVs

Above: **A Mk VII Churchill of an Independent Armoured Brigade. This version is armed with a 75mm gun which was an improvement on the 6 pdr. gun it replaced. It is easily recognisable by its circular exit hatches and its rectangular turret.**

Opposite: **An M 12, 155mm SP gun of the 434th Field Artillery Battalion, 7th US Armored Division. The M 12 GMC (Gun Motor Carriage) is constructed on the M3 Lee/Grant chassis, but the engine was moved nearer to the centre of the vehicle so as to leave space for the 155mm piece.**

Below: **A US Army M5A1 light tank. It has a large capacity stowage bin added at the rear, and "Applique" armour on the turret. Note the name 'Victory'.**

US M-10 TANK DESTROYER, 1943-45

An M-10 Tank Destroyer of the 899th Tank Destroyer Battalion, Tunisia 1943. This was the only American tank destroyer unit equipped with the M-10 on the theatre of operations. The vehicle bore no identification code, only the star on the turret. The tanks in the unit were going to receive a sand and olive drab camouflage but in fact it was not done.

M-10 'Richelieu II' of the 3e peloton de combat du 3e escadron du Régiment Blindé de Fusiliers Marins (RBFM) of the French 2e DB. This vehicle survived the conflict and took part in a parade in Paris, 18th June 1945.

An M-10 Tank Destroyer of the 6th US Armored Division, probably of the 691st TD Battalion, in the region of Karlsruhe, end of 1944 - beginning of 1945. The vehicle bears a large star on the forward glacis (see detail above) and it was possible therefore, that it was part of a unit which had recently arrived at the front.

ALLIED TANK DESTROYERS

An Achilles from an unknown British army unit. The sign *(see opposite)* seems to be that of an antitank unit. There are several interesting details: the additional front armour plate (30mm), which compensated for the weakness of the M 10, as well as the absence of headlights. Several of these vehicles were destroyed or captured by the 2. Panzerdivision.

An Achilles of the 2nd British Army in June 1944. With its 17 pounder gun the Achilles was a better tank destroyer than the American M 10 as far as its fire power was concerned. On the other hand, it had weak armour as well. All the Achilles guns were equipped with a counterweight.

Below: An M 10 of the 612th US Tank Destroyer Battalion in July 1944. This vehicle is the 18th vehicle of the A Company. The unit belonged to the 1st Army, the 3rd Army was only activated after the breakthrough of the 25th July.

A 18   1△ 612 TD

CORSAIR II

M-8 ARMORED CAR

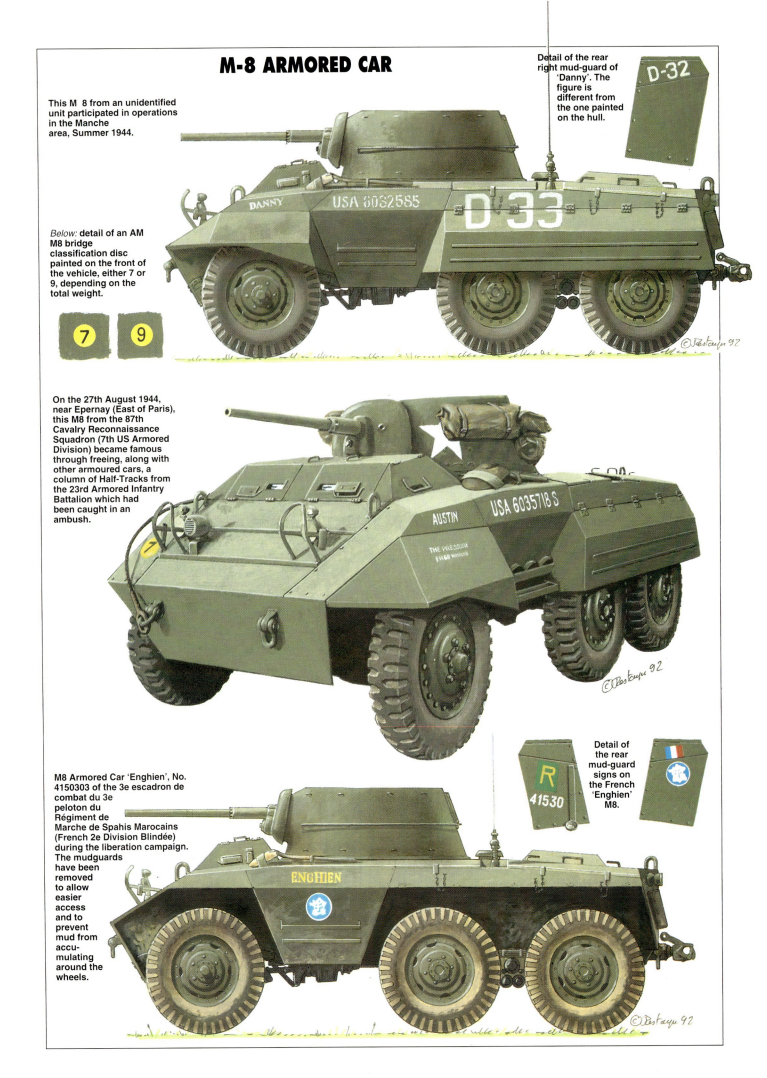

This M 8 from an unidentified unit participated in operations in the Manche area, Summer 1944.

Detail of the rear right mud-guard of 'Danny'. The figure is different from the one painted on the hull.

D-32

Below: detail of an AM M8 bridge classification disc painted on the front of the vehicle, either 7 or 9, depending on the total weight.

7 9

DANNY USA 6082585 D 33

On the 27th August 1944, near Epernay (East of Paris), this M8 from the 87th Cavalry Reconnaissance Squadron (7th US Armored Division) became famous through freeing, along with other armoured cars, a column of Half-Tracks from the 23rd Armored Infantry Battalion which had been caught in an ambush.

AUSTIN USA 6035718 S

THE PRESSURE FH60 MOU

M8 Armored Car 'Enghien', No. 4150303 of the 3e escadron de combat du 3e peloton du Régiment de Marche de Spahis Marocains (French 2e Division Blindée) during the liberation campaign. The mudguards have been removed to allow easier access and to prevent mud from accumulating around the wheels.

Detail of the rear mud-guard signs on the French 'Enghien' M8.

R 41530

ENGHIEN

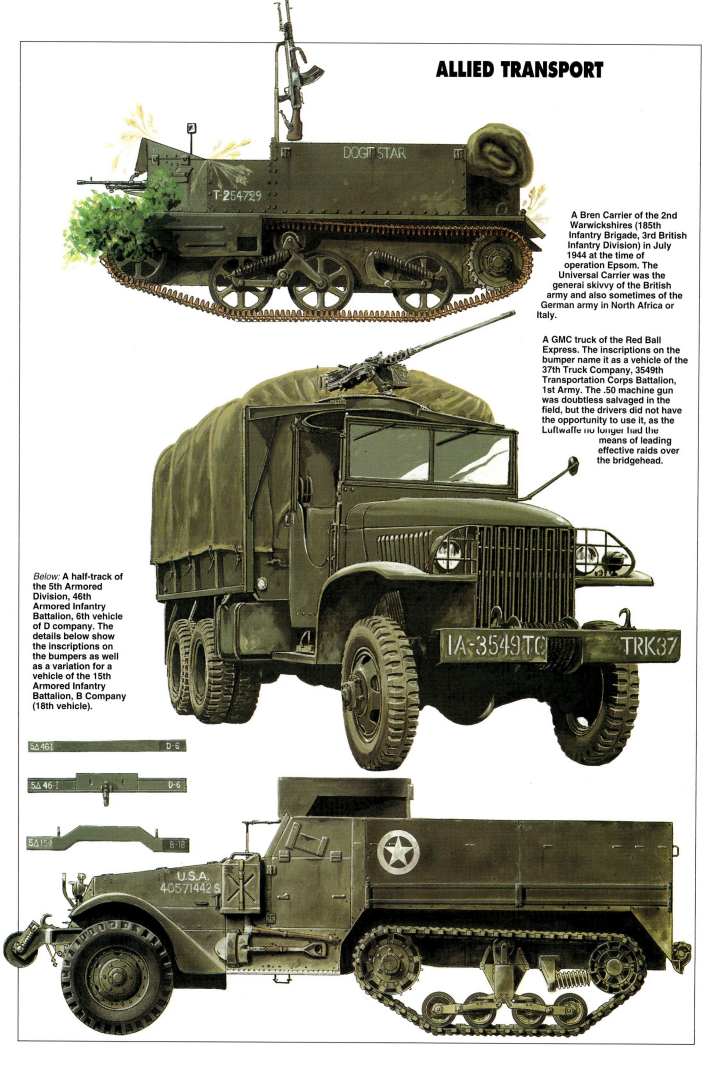

A Bren Carrier of the 2nd Warwickshires (185th Infantry Brigade, 3rd British Infantry Division) in July 1944 at the time of operation Epsom. The Universal Carrier was the general skivvy of the British army and also sometimes of the German army in North Africa or Italy.

A GMC truck of the Red Ball Express. The inscriptions on the bumper name it as a vehicle of the 37th Truck Company, 3549th Transportation Corps Battalion, 1st Army. The .50 machine gun was doubtless salvaged in the field, but the drivers did not have the opportunity to use it, as the Luftwaffe no longer had the means of leading effective raids over the bridgehead.

Below: **A half-track of the 5th Armored Division, 46th Armored Infantry Battalion, 6th vehicle of D company. The details below show the inscriptions on the bumpers as well as a variation for a vehicle of the 15th Armored Infantry Battalion, B Company (18th vehicle).**

1944-45 THE FALL OF THE REICH

TANKS AND PANZERJÄGER

A PzKpfW IV Ausf. H of the II. Abteilung of the 9. Panzerdivision in the Harz region, April 1945. On the 26th April 1945, after 68 months of combat, the division was disbanded. The black figures outlined in white were repainted in ochre or sand yellow for obvious reasons of discretion. The Panzer IV remained a formidable adversary right until the end.

A Tiger II of the 502. Schwere Panzer-Abteilung in the Eifel region. These survivors of the Ardennes offensive often fought alone in this region, and later at Boxberg and Kyllburg. It bears an ambush type camouflage and the surface was not covered with zimmerit.

Panzerjäger 38 (Hetzer) of an autonomous Panzerjäger Abteilung. These units consisted of two companies each of 17 vehicles and 5 Hetzer for the Stab. The very reliable Hetzer was used by both the Swiss and Swedish armies until well after the war. Note the absence of any mark of nationality on this model.

PANTHER AND JAGDPANTHER AGAINST THE BRITISH

A Panther Ausf. G of the I. Abteilung of the 11. Panzerdivision in the region of Reichenbach mid-April 1945. The return of Spring meant leafy branches could be used for camouflage against allied aviation, still prevalent at that time. On the 7th/8th March 1945, the 11. Panzerdivision only had 25 tanks operational.

A Panther Ausf. G of the I. Abteilung of the 116. Panzerdivision, with the ambush type camouflage typical of the end of the war. It was not rare to see inexperienced crews with Panthers and even Jagdpanthers and Jagdtigers, whereas the veterans had to work miracles with the PzKpfW IV and the Sturmgeschütze. This was a typical aberration of the German command at that time; they believed that good equipment could compensate for lack of experience.

A Jagdpanther of the 3. Kompanie of the I. Abteilung of the Panzer Lehr Regiment 130. In February 1945, this unit used Jagdpanther within its 3. Kompanie, the 1. and 2. Kompanies on the other hand, had Panthers. Towards the end of the war the proportion of assault guns compared with tanks became larger.

GERMAN TANK DESTROYERS

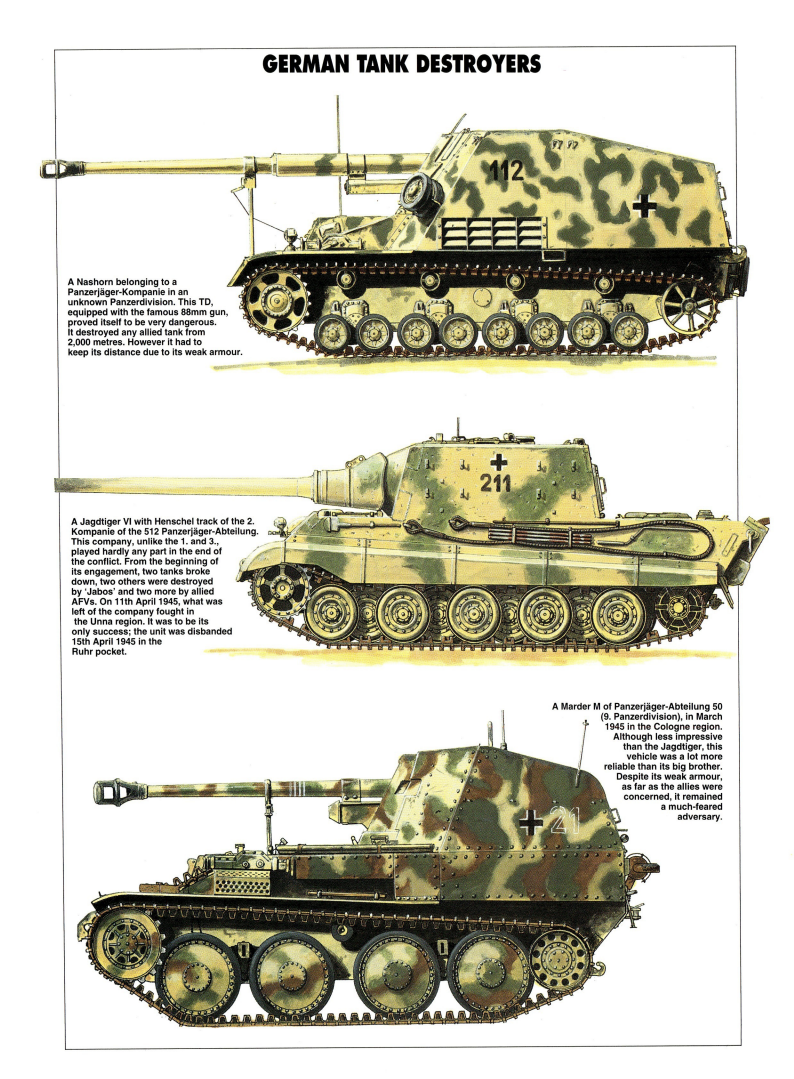

A Nashorn belonging to a Panzerjäger-Kompanie in an unknown Panzerdivision. This TD, equipped with the famous 88mm gun, proved itself to be very dangerous. It destroyed any allied tank from 2,000 metres. However it had to keep its distance due to its weak armour.

A Jagdtiger VI with Henschel track of the 2. Kompanie of the 512 Panzerjäger-Abteilung. This company, unlike the 1. and 3., played hardly any part in the end of the conflict. From the beginning of its engagement, two tanks broke down, two others were destroyed by 'Jabos' and two more by allied AFVs. On 11th April 1945, what was left of the company fought in the Unna region. It was to be its only success; the unit was disbanded 15th April 1945 in the Ruhr pocket.

A Marder M of Panzerjäger-Abteilung 50 (9. Panzerdivision), in March 1945 in the Cologne region. Although less impressive than the Jagdtiger, this vehicle was a lot more reliable than its big brother. Despite its weak armour, as far as the allies were concerned, it remained a much-feared adversary.

STURMGESCHÜTZE AND PANZERJÄGER

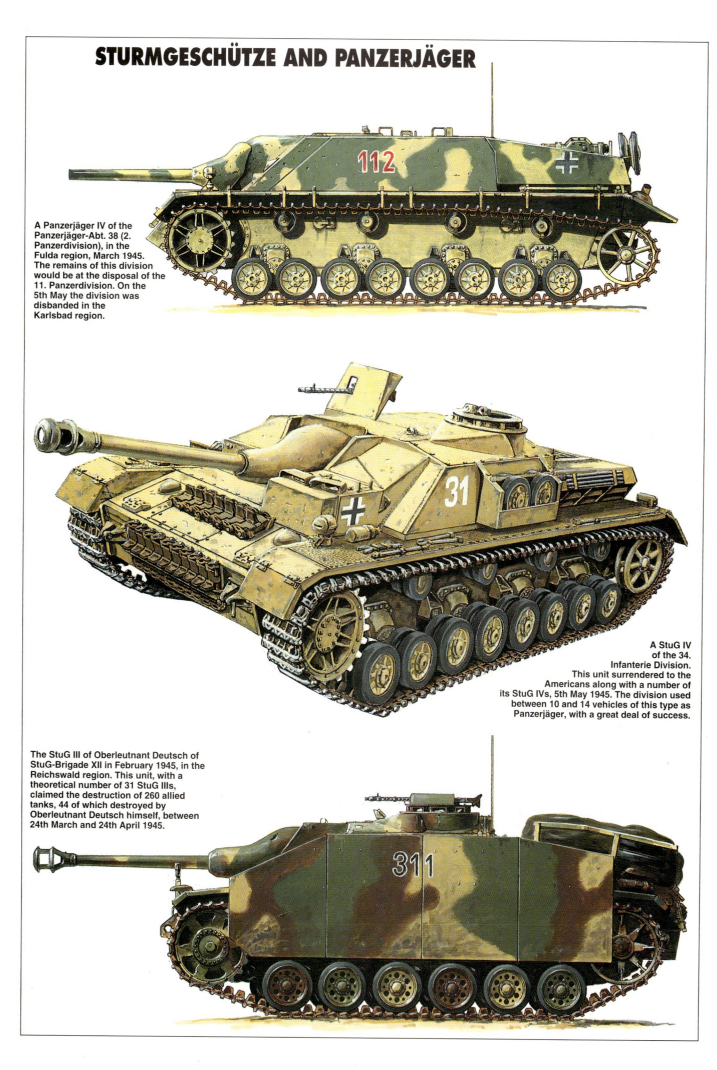

A Panzerjäger IV of the Panzerjäger-Abt. 38 (2. Panzerdivision), in the Fulda region, March 1945. The remains of this division would be at the disposal of the 11. Panzerdivision. On the 5th May the division was disbanded in the Karlsbad region.

A StuG IV of the 34. Infanterie Division. This unit surrendered to the Americans along with a number of its StuG IVs, 5th May 1945. The division used between 10 and 14 vehicles of this type as Panzerjäger, with a great deal of success.

The StuG III of Oberleutnant Deutsch of StuG-Brigade XII in February 1945, in the Reichswald region. This unit, with a theoretical number of 31 StuG IIIs, claimed the destruction of 260 allied tanks, 44 of which destroyed by Oberleutnant Deutsch himself, between 24th March and 24th April 1945.

GERMAN TANK DESTROYERS

A Hetzer tank destroyer, built on a Panzer 38 (t) chassis. This vehicle belonged to the Panzerjäger-Abteilung of lieutenant-colonel Schulz, which became well known in the battle of Koenigsbach in April 1945.

A Sturmgeschütz from an unknown Volksgrenadierdivision, defending the Pforzheim region in the Würtemburg plain, April 1945.

Jagdtiger of the 1. Kp. of Panzerjäger-Abteilung 653, commanded by Major Fromme, in the Hockenheim region, on the banks of the Rhine. The tactical number is assumed, but its position and colour are confirmed.

GERMAN TANK DESTROYERS AND SELF-PROPELLED GUNS

A Sturmtiger belonging to Kompanie 1000 and attached to the artillery regiment of a German division, very probably the 16. Volksgrenadierdivision. These huge vehicles often encountered setbacks during operations and the majority of them were abandoned by their crews.

A Jagdpanther V of Panzerjäger-Abteilung 654. This unit, based partly in Alsace and partly in Germany, fought the 1st French Army for several months. Note the very characteristic appearance of the zimmerit.

A Nashorn from an unidentified s. Heeres Panzerjäger-Abteilung. The Nashorn carried an 88mm gun on a Panzer IV chassis.

FRENCH AND GERMAN TANKS

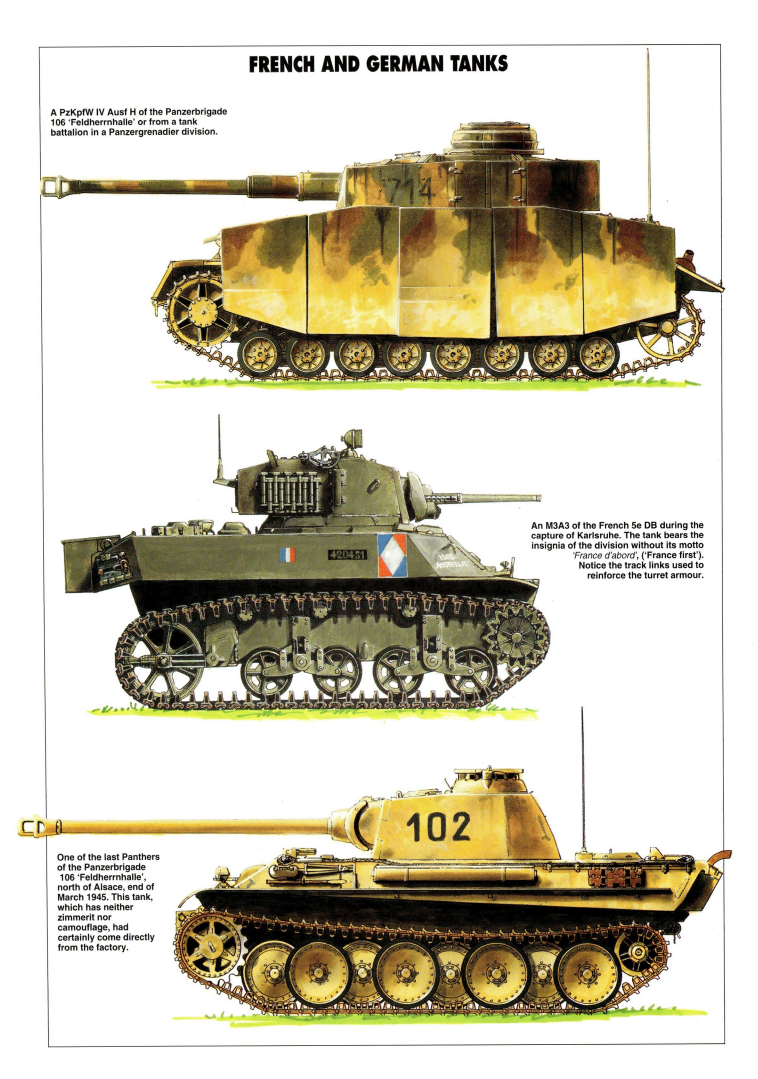

A PzKpfW IV Ausf H of the Panzerbrigade 106 'Feldherrnhalle' or from a tank battalion in a Panzergrenadier division.

An M3A3 of the French 5e DB during the capture of Karlsruhe. The tank bears the insignia of the division without its motto *'France d'abord'*, (**'France first'**). Notice the track links used to reinforce the turret armour.

One of the last Panthers of the Panzerbrigade 106 'Feldherrnhalle', north of Alsace, end of March 1945. This tank, which has neither zimmerit nor camouflage, had certainly come directly from the factory.

M4 SHERMANS OF THE FRENCH 2e DB

'Romilly', an M4A3 of the 2e compagnie du 501e RCC (régiment de chars de combat). Registration No. 420 613, this tank is principally known for its entry into Paris with the 'Champaubert' and 'Montmirail', the night of 24th and 25th August 1944.

'Reims II', an M4A3 of the 2e peloton du 2e escadron du 12e régiment de cuirassiers.

'Flandres', an M4A3 Sherman equipped with a turret for a 76mm M1A1 gun. This tank belonged to the 12th régiment de chasseurs d'Afrique.

TANKS AND TANK DESTROYERS OF THE FRENCH 2e DB

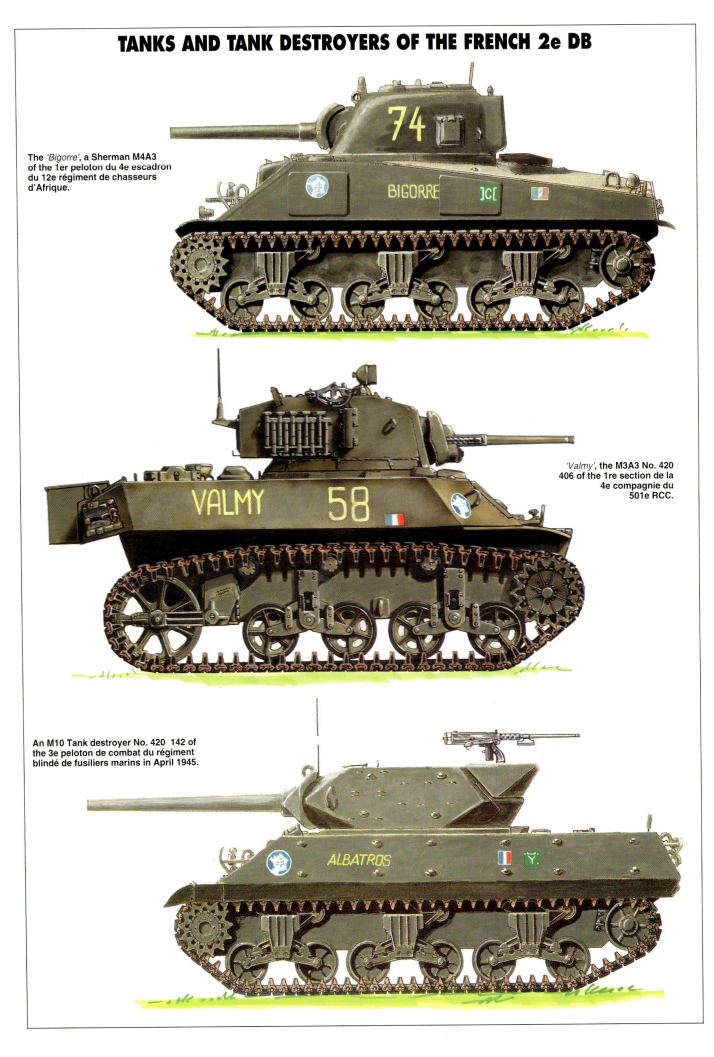

The 'Bigorre', a Sherman M4A3 of the 1er peloton du 4e escadron du 12e régiment de chasseurs d'Afrique.

'Valmy', the M3A3 No. 420 406 of the 1re section de la 4e compagnie du 501e RCC.

An M10 Tank destroyer No. 420 142 of the 3e peloton de combat du régiment blindé de fusiliers marins in April 1945.

ARMOURED VEHICLES OF THE FRENCH 2e DB

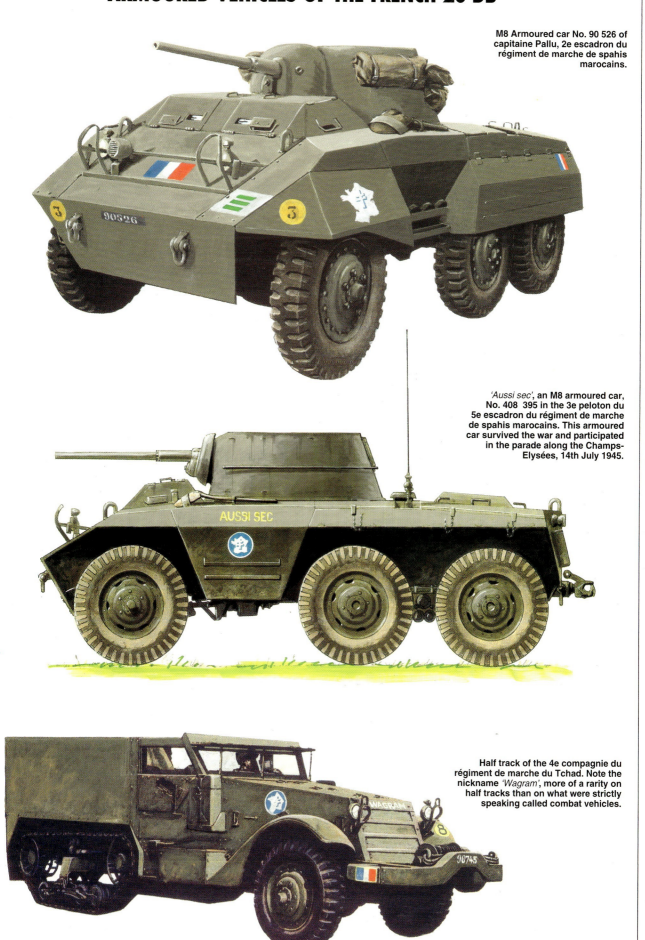

M8 Armoured car No. 90 526 of capitaine Pallu, 2e escadron du régiment de marche de spahis marocains.

'Aussi sec', an M8 armoured car, No. 408 395 in the 3e peloton du 5e escadron du régiment de marche de spahis marocains. This armoured car survived the war and participated in the parade along the Champs-Elysées, 14th July 1945.

Half track of the 4e compagnie du régiment de marche du Tchad. Note the nickname 'Wagram', more of a rarity on half tracks than on what were strictly speaking called combat vehicles.

TANKS AND ARMOURED VEHICLES OF THE FRENCH 5e DB

'Montcalm', a Sherman of the 4/5e RCA (régiment de chasseurs d'Afrique) during the capture of Baden-Baden. This is an absolutely standard M4A3 but the large characters of the name of this tank were specific to the 5e RCA, perhaps even to the 4e peloton.

An M10 Tank destroyer of the 7e RCA. Unlike many M10s of the French 1re armée, this one bears a French registration number and a cross of Lorraine.

A half track of the 5e DB, Combat Command 6, during its advance on Breitenholtz, 19th April 1945.

M4 SHERMAN OF THE FRENCH 5e DB

The *'Loup II'*, an M4A3 of the 2e escadron du 1er cuirassiers. This tank won fame at the battle of Koenigsbach by destroying a Hetzer.

The *'Bombarde'*, a Sherman from an unknown unit of the 5e DB. The X2 mark is rare and its meaning remains a mystery.

The *'Chasseur Brachet'*, an M4A3 Sherman of the 6e RCA. This tank was destroyed at Küppingen, on the road to Stuttgart, by an 88mm shell, 18th April 1945.

ALLIED ARMOURED VEHICLES AND TANKS

Belonging to the 14th Armoured Division, this half-track was seen in the Bare region in November 1944. This vehicle was on the strength of an anti-tank unit. Details of the nickname *'Baby Bastard N° 1'* are given in the close-up. The vehicle's serial number is only speculative.

An M 8 self-propelled Howitzer from 3e RCA as seen during operations to the south of Rosenau on the Rhine bank.

An M 10 tank destroyer from 9e RCA during the Belfort breakthrough. In appalling weather conditions, the hull of the vehicle had to be crudely daubed with white paint so as to better match the snowy landscape.

AMERICAN RECCE AND ARMOURED VEHICLES

An M 8 armoured car from 92nd Cavalry Reconnaissance Squadron, 12th Armoured Division. This M 8 was the fourth vehicle of the command platoon.

The sixth vehicle from A Company, 12th Armored Division was probably an M4A3, even though this can not be ascertained from this three-quarter view.

An M4A3 Sherman (76mm gun) from the 14th Armoured Division. Gun barrel markings were only used by 12th and 14th Armoured Division armour (even though less frequently by the latter). This tank is the second vehicle from B Company, 25th Tank Battalion.

2e DIVISION BLINDÉE VEHICLES AND ARMOUR

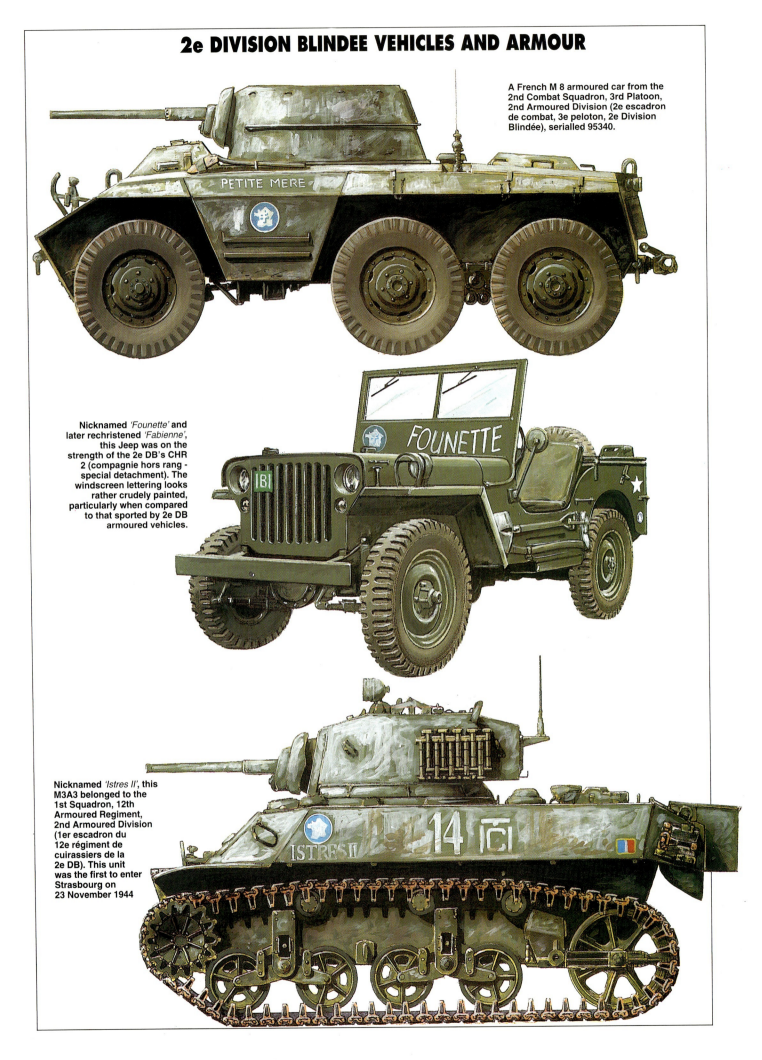

A French M 8 armoured car from the 2nd Combat Squadron, 3rd Platoon, 2nd Armoured Division (2e escadron de combat, 3e peloton, 2e Division Blindée), serialled 95340.

Nicknamed *'Founette'* and later rechristened *'Fabienne'*, this Jeep was on the strength of the 2e DB's CHR 2 (compagnie hors rang - special detachment). The windscreen lettering looks rather crudely painted, particularly when compared to that sported by 2e DB armoured vehicles.

Nicknamed *'Istres II'*, this M3A3 belonged to the 1st Squadron, 12th Armoured Regiment, 2nd Armoured Division (1er escadron du 12e régiment de cuirassiers de la 2e DB). This unit was the first to enter Strasbourg on 23 November 1944

AMERICAN ARMOUR IN FRENCH MARKINGS

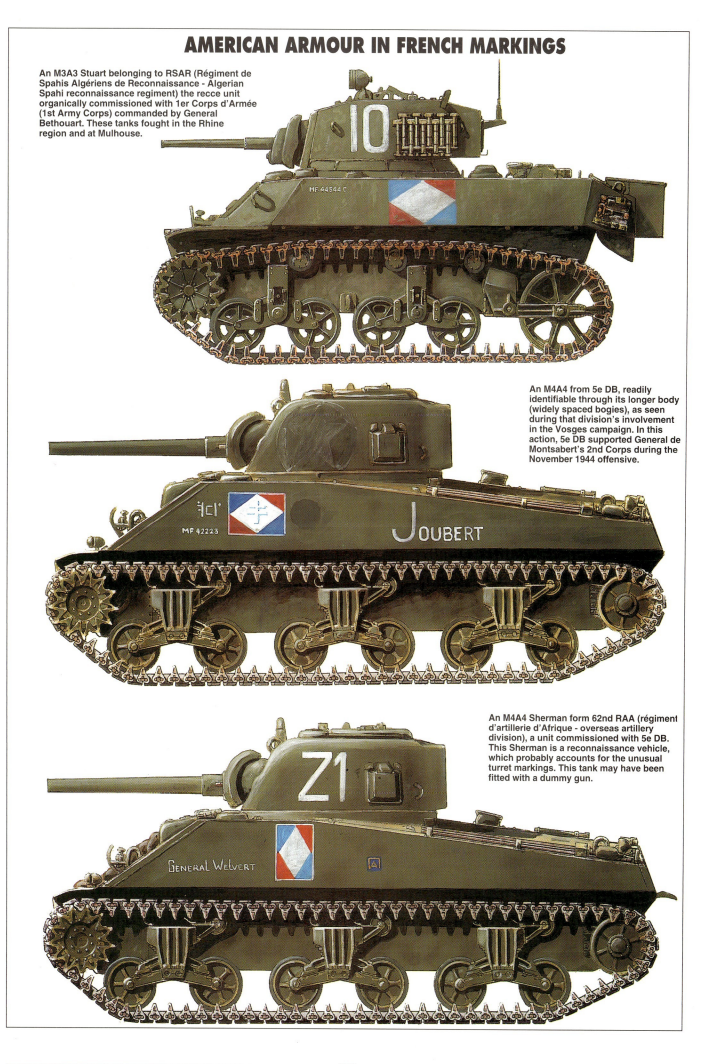

An M3A3 Stuart belonging to RSAR (Régiment de Spahis Algériens de Reconnaissance - Algerian Spahi reconnaissance regiment) the recce unit organically commissioned with 1er Corps d'Armée (1st Army Corps) commanded by General Bethouart. These tanks fought in the Rhine region and at Mulhouse.

An M4A4 from 5e DB, readily identifiable through its longer body (widely spaced bogies), as seen during that division's involvement in the Vosges campaign. In this action, 5e DB supported General de Montsabert's 2nd Corps during the November 1944 offensive.

An M4A4 Sherman form 62nd RAA (régiment d'artillerie d'Afrique - overseas artillery division), a unit commissioned with 5e DB. This Sherman is a reconnaissance vehicle, which probably accounts for the unusual turret markings. This tank may have been fitted with a dummy gun.

BRITISH TANKS

A Sherman Firefly of the 11th Armoured Division, during operation Plunder, beginning of April 1945. The figure 51 on a red background a code number which identified the arm and the type of unit to which the vehicle belonged. This tank belonged to the first tank regiment of an armoured formation, in this case the 23rd Hussars.

A Churchill of the 34th Independent Armoured Brigade in April 1945. This brigade fought as a support for the 6th Battalion, The Royal Welch Fusiliers (53rd 'Wessex' Division), during operation Veritable. The Churchill very quickly became stuck in waterlogged terrain because of its immense weight, therefore its role in the battle was insignificant.

A Cromwell of the Guards Armoured Division near Xanten, March 1945. The code number (left) 52, indicates that the tank belonged to the second regiment of the armoured brigade of the division, here the 1st Coldstream Guards. In the last weeks of the war, a large number of Cromwells were replaced by their successor, the infinitely superior Comet. 'The ever open eye', symbol of the division, is illustrated above left.

AMERICAN LIGHT TANKS AND TANK DESTROYERS

8△80△ D7

An M24 Chaffee light tank of D company, 80th Tank Battalion, 8th Armored Division, in the Harz region, April 1945. Its 75mm gun, the same used in some B25 bombers, did not have the same penetrative power as the Sherman's. On the other hand, it was clearly superior to the 37mm of the M5. In spite of its light armour (25mm), the M24 was a good light tank.

Below: detail of tactical marks on this tank.

An M5A1 of the 12th Armored Division, end of March 1945, in the Gemersheim-Würzburg region. The division had just participated in the elimination of the German pocket of the Saar-Palatinate triangle, what Bradley called the most successful American operation of the war. By March 1945 though, the M5A1 was completely outmatched.

USA 3089898 S   SHANTY IRISH

7△ 636TD   A11

An M18 Hellcat Tank Destroyer of the 7th Armored Division, 636th TD Battalion, A Company, in the Bonn region, March 1945. At this time, the division neutralised the last German defences on the banks of the Rhine, between Remagen and Bonn. The Hellcat, with its 90mm gun and its stocky outline, was an excellent tank destroyer, but in 1945, the idea of tank destroyers did not have a great deal of support in the US Army.

Below: detail of the tactical marks of this tank.

US ARMY M4 SHERMANS

AN M4A3E8 Sherman of the 14th Armored Division, 25th Tank Battalion, C Company, end of April 1945 in the town of Eichstatt. The 'Easy 8', as the Sherman with HVSS suspension was nicknamed, was the best version of the Sherman in operation during the second world war. All the same, this model is covered with sandbags which offered extra protection against the German Panzerfaust and Panzerschreck portable antitank rocket launchers.

'Charly', an M4A1 (76mm) of the 69th Tank Battalion of the 6th Armored Division, in the Oppenheim region, 25th March 1945, when the division was crossing the Rhine to forge ahead to Main. The installation of a 76mm gun made a change of turret necessary. On the other hand, the cast body of the M4A1 remained unchanged.

An M4A3 of the 12th Armored Division, 714th Tank Battalion, D Company in the Speyer region, March 1945. Towards the end of the war, more recent and better armed models started to take the place of the M4A3 within the Armored Divisions. Its gun was acknowledged to be insufficient against the Panzer.

ALLIED TANKS AND AFVs

An M3A1 Armored Personnel Carrier of the 9th US Armored Division, 60th Armored Infantry Battalion, C Company, near Frankfurt, March 1945. This division was famous for capturing the Ludendorff bridge at Remagen, 7th March 1945. *Above:* detail of the marks situated on the bumpers of the vehicle.

Below: variation for another vehicle, from A company.

A Comet of the 11th British Armoured Division during the last weeks of the conflict.

The Comet was an improved version of the Cromwell with a 17 Pdr short gun conceived by Vickers for the small turret of the new tank. The first ones reached the theatre of operations in December 1944, in the Ardennes, then in greater number, also for the 11th Armoured Division, some time in 1945. The Comet was without doubt the best British tank of the war, but it arrived a little late...

An M10 of the 701st US Tank Destroyer Battalion, C Company, attached to the 5th US Armored Division in the Tangermünde region, on the Elbe, April 1945. The Americans chose to wait for the Russians on this river, as it was a wide, natural barrier which could not be missed: the two allies would therefore be forced to meet one another. During the last months of the war, the M10 crews all waited impatiently to be equipped with the M36 and especially the M18 Hellcat.

Publishing Manager : Patrick RIVIÈRE.
Design and layout : Patrick LESIEUR. © PLST
Translation : Julia Finel.

ISBN : 2 908 182 37 6.
Publishers number's : 2-908182.
Publishers by **Histoire & Collections**
5, avenue de la République
75541 Paris Cedex 11
Tél. : (1) 40 21 18 20
Fax : (1) 47 00 51 11

Editorial composition : Macintosh Quadra 800, X'Press and Adobe Illustrator.

Photography : SCIPE, Paris

Printed by Imprimerie France Quercy, 46001 Cahors. France on 2nd trimester 1996.